YOU COULD DO SOMETHING AMAZING WITH YOUR LIFE
[YOU ARE RAOUL MOAT]

ANDREW
HANKINSON

YOU COULD DO SOMETHING AMAZING WITH YOUR LIFE [YOU ARE RAOUL MOAT]

SCRIBE
Melbourne • London

Scribe Publications
18-20 Edward St, Brunswick, Victoria 3056, Australia
2 John St, Clerkenwell, London, WC1N 2ES, United Kingdom

First published by Scribe 2016
This edition published 2017

Typeset in Adobe Garamond by the publishers
Printed and bound in the UK by CPI Group (UK) Ltd, Croydon CR0 4YY

Scribe Publications is committed to the sustainable use of natural resources
and the use of paper products made responsibly from those resources.

9781925106558 (Australian paperback)
9781911344322 (UK paperback)
9781925113754 (e-book)

CIP records for this title are available from the British Library
and the National Library of Australia

scribepublications.com.au
scribepublications.co.uk

To my wife and children

A questionnaire arrives from the Regional Department of Psychotherapy. There are seventeen pages of questions. They want you to complete your answers and send it back before your first appointment with a psychologist.

It's 2008. You sit in the house and write your surname, first name, date of birth, address, age and telephone number. On the next page you describe your symptoms,

I FEEL TIRED, ANXIOUS, ISOLATED, HELPLESS, ANGRY. I FIND IT DIFFICULT TO SLEEP OR RELAX

It asks how these symptoms affect your life. You write,

THEY STOP MY LIFE FROM PROGRESSING CON-
STRUCTIVELY. I AM AGGRESSIVE AND VIOLENT
OUTSIDE THE HOME IF PROVOKED

It asks why you think this happens. You write about the bad parts of your childhood, police harassment, having no family support, worrying about your children's future, and feeling alone.

It asks what you enjoy and what your achievements have been.

I ENJOY BEING A DAD. MY CHILDREN ARE MY GREAT-
EST ACHIEVEMENT. HAVING THE MORALS I HAVE.
NOT LOSING THE PLOT AND BEING IN JAIL. I ENJOY
MY RELATIONSHIP

It asks what you've found most difficult in life and what has brought the least satisfaction.

KEEPING MY COOL HAS BEEN MOST DIFFICULT. NOT
GIVING MY KIDS AND GIRLFRIEND A BETTER LIFE
WITH ME

It asks about your family history. You write that your father is *UNKNOWN*. You write your mum's name and age. In the siblings box you write *ANGUS*. For his occupation and marital status you put *UNKNOWN*. It asks about your relationship with your dad. You write *STEPFATHER* and underline it. You write five lines about him. It asks about your relationship with your mum. You write nine lines.

2

On the next page it says,

It would help us to know something of your background. Could you tell us something about your childhood and family including any changes or separations that you experienced? Were any relationships especially important to you, for example with brothers, sisters, grandparents, aunts or uncles?

You write,

LOOK, I'M NOW REALLY PISSED OFF BECAUSE THESE QUESTIONS SHOULD BE DISCUSSED IN PERSON, AWAY FROM MY MRS AND KIDS, SO THEY DON'T HAVE TO SEE ME WOUND UP ABOUT THINGS I CHOOSE TO NOT THINK ABOUT. I CAN EXPRESS MYSELF BETTER IN PERSON AND SEE THIS AS TOTALLY DISMISSIVE AND UNCARING, AND WAS ABOUT TO CHUCK THESE FORMS IN THE BIN, BUT WROTE THIS COS I NEED THE HELP. IT IS GOING TO TAKE AN EFFORT FOR ME TO DO ALL THIS, SO CONTACT ME AND I'LL DISCUSS WHATEVER YOU WANT. I DO NOT WISH TO DISCUSS MY LIFE WITH PAPER

You turn the page.

It asks about your schools. You list them.

It asks about previous employment.

3

ENGINEERING (MECHANICAL). DOOR SUPERVISOR. MECHANIC

It asks about current employment.

UNEMPLOYED AT PRESENT. COULD DO EXTREMELY WELL IF THE POLICE DID NOT PUT THE MIX IN SO MUCH, DESPITE NOT EVEN HAVING A CAUTION TO MY NAME. STRONG EVIDENCE TO BACK THIS UP

It asks about difficulties at work. You leave it blank.

The next page is domestic life. You write that you've been living with Sam for three years. She's nineteen years old. It asks about your previous significant relationships. You put that you were seeing Marissa from 1998 until 2004. She's the mother of your two eldest children. You write that you have three children and Sam is the mother of the youngest. You describe your relationship as extremely loving and rewarding.

The next page asks about your relationship with Sam. You write that it's strong and there are no worrying problems. She's honest, faithful and decent. You write that there isn't much space to put all the good stuff in here. For the bad stuff you put,

CAN RELY ON ME TOO MUCH, AND BELIEVES I CAN TAKE ON THE WORLD AND FIX EVERYTHING

4

The next section is health. You write that you have asthma and need more help with it. You write that there was a recent accident where your hand got crushed, shattering the bones. It has not healed properly and doesn't work properly. It looks terrible.

You don't drink or take non-prescribed drugs.

It asks,

Have you ever tried to harm yourself in any way?

YES

You underline it twice.

2 OVERDOSES

It asks if you've had psychiatric treatment or care in the past.

NO

It asks if you've had counselling or psychotherapy.

YES. COLLINGWOOD COURT FOR 12 MONTHS AS REFERRED BY DOCTOR

Can you say what it is about yourself that you want to change?

I DON'T WISH TO CHANGE ANYTHING. HAVE A

5

CALMER FRAME OF MIND AND EMOTIONAL STATE MAYBE

It asks how you expect the treatment to help and what form you imagine it taking.

I HAVE NO IDEA. KNOWING MY LUCK IT WILL BE ALL STRAIGHT JACKETS, ELECTRICITY TO THE HEAD AND A CAGE

The final page asks for any other information. You leave it blank.

You send the questionnaire back to them.

A few days later a letter arrives. You've got an appointment with a trainee clinical psychologist on April 29, 2008.

You don't attend.

Another letter arrives. It says they don't normally reschedule appointments, but they know this is hard for you, so they're offering you another appointment. It's on May 13, 2008.

You don't attend.

You are discharged from the waiting list.

Two years later you shoot three people and shoot yourself. You will be called a monster. You will be called evil. The prime minister, David Cameron, will stand up in Parliament and say you were a callous murderer, end of story. You have nine days and your whole life to prove you are more than a callous murderer.

Go.

YOU WILL DIE IN EIGHT DAYS

They release you from prison at 10.55am. The North East is bright and sunny [as it often isn't]. Your mission [as you explained it to another prisoner] is to get the gun, shoot Sam, shoot her new boyfriend, shoot Sam's mum for trying to split you up, shoot the social worker who pissed you off, shoot the psychiatrist for giving you a negative report [though you can't remember their name] and point the gun at the police until they shoot you.

Stevie [a friend] picks you up at Durham Prison and drives you to Fenham [a suburb in the West End of Newcastle upon Tyne]. The local bricks are red. There are green trees and gardens. You live at 128 Fenham Hall Drive, a semi-detached [council] house with a garden and a bus stop outside the front gate — which you wrote to the council to complain about, because junkies hang around the bus stop injecting heroin and throwing needles over your wall, crowds of school kids make access to your property hazardous, teenagers congregate there at night to drink, swear, fight and abuse, someone destroyed your £565 leylandii, and the covert camera in your hedge recorded drunken teenagers having sex in your garden, Lambrini bottles getting thrown at your house, and people vandalising your vehicles and the bus stop, footage and stills of which you handed to Northumbria Police [at the end of the letter you add that you want to build a driveway and getting planning permission would be easier if they moved the bus stop].

Stevie drops you off. You look around. It doesn't feel like home anymore. The garden is overgrown. Maybe you've come out of prison a different kid. You walk inside. Karl appears with his girlfriend [Tara]. You say hello. They say hello.

Karl's a good friend [his full name's Karl Ness and he's twenty-six years old]. He does odd jobs for you. He's been staying at your house to feed the dogs, pay the bills and keep things tidy, but everything looks dirty and unkempt. He passes you the phone. He stashed the gun at Lana's house, Tara's daughter [he hid it secretly, without telling them]. He's going to get it.

Karl and Tara leave. It's lunchtime. You don't feel like eating. You haven't felt like eating for weeks. You walk across the road to the barber's and ask for a Mohican, like Robert De Niro in *Taxi Driver*. The barber starts to cut your hair. You look in the mirror. Your face is tired and gaunt. You don't look well. Prison made you ill. You tell the barber and anyone listening that you've just done a stretch and will probably be back inside by Friday [tomorrow] because you've got arses to kick [nobody laughs].

The barber finishes your hair. You walk home and sit on the couch. Karl gets back with the gun. It's in a blue bag. You take it out. It's an old sawn-off shotgun, double-barrelled, with one barrel over the other. Karl sorted it out while you were inside [you supervised via the prison phone, being careful as you knew the calls were recorded]. The cartridges are in the bag.

You drive to town, which is only five minutes away. You park on Grey Street [in the city centre] and walk to Bagnall & Kirkwood [a gun and tackle shop] where you buy fishing weights [at 2.09pm] — just small metal spheres, like ball bearings.

You drive home. Karl and Sean are in the street [Sean is Karl's friend; his real name's Qhuram Awan; he's a twenty-three-year-old bouncer; you've met him a few times]. They load your BMW onto the recovery truck. They're taking it to get repaired because Karl, like a monkey in a rocket ship, put normal cooking oil in it rather than the special biodiesel you manufacture in the garden. You help them load it onto the truck and go inside.

You call Sam. Sometimes it's hard to get a signal in the house because of the lead-lined bricks, but you get through and she answers, but she won't listen. She just goes on about the puppies, saying how she can't look after them so Karl needs to go to her house and pick them up, but you can't go over there, and she shouts and hangs up, and you're left thinking: Is this a bad dream? Where's Sam gone? She was your best friend. Who was

11

that? And you sit on the couch using a lock-knife to open the plastic casings of some of the shotgun cartridges. You remove the shot and put a fishing weight inside instead. You take some of the powder out too. You seal the casings back up and wonder how somebody who had it all ended up in a situation like this, everything just a pile of chaos.

You phone the GP and book an appointment for Monday [nobody knows why]. Karl gets back. He's fixed the BMW. He sits on the other couch. You Google Sam's new boyfriend. You know he teaches karate, and you guess the classes are somewhere near Sam's new house [she lives in Birtley, just over the river, south of Gateshead].

You type on the laptop,

taekwondo Birtley

Chester le street martial arts

martial arts clubs durham

You get the names of five possible dojos [church halls and sports centres] as well as instructors. It's hard to know the right one. Maybe it's this one, William McElhone [it isn't]. You call Birtley Leisure Centre for confirmation, but they're no help, so you write the addresses on a piece of paper and hand it to Karl and walk out to the van [at 7pm] with the gun in a bin-liner. Karl programs the addresses into the TomTom and you drive

12

onto the A1, over the river, past the Metrocentre, turning off by the Angel of the North. Karl's phone keeps beeping. It's Tara. He texts back and calls her a psycho.

You drive to each dojo and do your recon, but it's getting late [10pm] and all the classes have finished, so you abort the mission and drive to Tesco's car park for a debrief [in Chester-le-Street, a small town three miles south of Birtley]. Karl wants to see Tara, who's at Lana's house, so you drive to Lana's in Lemington [back over the river, in the West End of Newcastle]. You go inside and Tara and Lana are in the sitting room. You tell them what Sam's done to you and how she's changed. Lana says you just need a good night out, but no, that's not it. Karl drives you home.

...

It's 11pm. You call Anth [Anthony Wright; you met him at a gym fourteen years ago and worked on the doors together; now he owns a garage in Byker; you earn money by using your recovery truck to drop off vehicles there; he's thirty-four years old]. You talk to him for two hours. He's your best friend and he's been here for you before, particularly last year, when Sam moved out. It had you in bits, that. She left while you were at work, just disappeared and switched her phone off, giving you no option but to track her down, which you did, because there was stuff on Facebook, and you found out she was at her gran's house and you drove down there and sat outside, but she wouldn't come out, not until Anth got on the phone to her,

13

and even then, when she came out [you had the gun on the passenger seat], she still wouldn't agree to move back in, but Anth is always there for you, which you tried to say thank you for in the letter you wrote, back when things got bad [*sorry for being a tit*] but you never gave it to him [it was a suicide note], just like you never gave the others their letters, like the one to Karl [*all tools etc are yours if you want*], and one to Richard [*you're a good mate*], another for Duncan [*you are welcome to whichever dog you want*], one to the council asking them to look after your kids [*I have failed them both and don't wish to do so any longer*], and the longest to Sam [*I don't know what to say except I love you, always have and always will*]. That night, when Sam wouldn't move back in, Anth says he tried to call you, but you'd switched your phone off, so he thought you'd gone ahead with it [killed yourself], but eventually Sam agreed to see you. The point is, Anth helped a lot, because he knows your one weakness is women [you once visited a hypnotist to get over a girlfriend dumping you], but this time it's not like that. It's more than that. He can tell you're depressed. Your voice is breaking. You're thirty-seven years old, too old to start again. You've come out of prison with nothing. And for the first time he doesn't have an answer. Tonight is unpleasant.

...

...

There's an attic upstairs. You were going to convert it into an office. And you told the girls you'd convert it into a dream bedroom for them. Not anymore. There's a noose up there.

...

...

You're not going to kill yourself tonight. You'll give it one last try with Sam. It's you and her against the world.

...

You can't sleep. You've always had trouble sleeping. You used to spend sleepless nights playing Xbox or looking through the keeping box of cards from the kids, watching the shopping channel, or the Mr Bean DVD, the one where he gets sent to an art gallery in America and they think he's a boffin, but he hasn't got a clue really. He ends up sneezing on Whistler's *Mother*, and when he tries to rub it off with turps the painting blisters up, and they have a grand unveiling, but there's just this terrible hand-drawn picture that he's done instead of the masterpiece. It's hilarious. You don't always sit and laugh all the way through a film, but that's one of the funniest things you've seen, definitely as good as Laurel & Hardy, which is the kind of humour you like, especially *Them Thar Hills*, which is their classic, where they get in a fight and double-team this guy by putting treacle down his pants. You like that sort of thing much more than modern humour, which you don't get at all, though a mate sends you jokes all the time, and he's not a racist, but there's one he sent you about two Pakistanis in a people-carrier

15

who have a fatal crash on the A1, and there's outrage because there were five spare seats.

Ha

Another joke that's stuck in your head over the years is about a tramp sitting in front of a jewellery shop. Suddenly an elephant comes along and kicks the shutter down, sucks up all the jewels through its trunk, and escapes down the street. A policeman turns up and asks the tramp if he saw anything. The tramp says, yes, he saw an elephant do it, and the policeman asks what the elephant looked like. The tramp says it just looked like an elephant. So the policeman says,

Well, there's two types of elephant. An African elephant has big ears and an Indian elephant has little ears. What kind was it?

And the tramp says,

Well, how are you supposed to tell if it's wearing a balaclava?

Ha ha ha

And there's this other one, about a Pakistani who arrives in England, and as he's going through customs a guard comes over and gives him a hundred grand to welcome him to the country.

There you go, there's a hundred grand.

In the next queue someone from the housing department comes over and gives him a house,

There you go, there's a house.

In the next queue someone from the job centre comes over and says,

There you go, there's a job.

At the final desk the Pakistani gets a stamp in his passport saying he's officially an English citizen now, so all the departments come over and take it all back, saying,

Nah, you get fuck all.

Ha

...

...

You haven't slept for weeks. You couldn't sleep more than an hour a night in prison. It was harder than you expected, harder than the public thinks, surrounded by junkies and scum, locked in a tiny cell for twenty-three hours a day with people dropping like flies around you. In a single week one slit his throat, one cut his wrists and another hanged himself, because they couldn't hack the consequences of one mistake [the

17

Ministry of Justice recorded one apparent self-inflicted death and forty-six incidents of self-harm at Durham Prison while you were there]. You kept busy, weight training, helping other kids train, and you got a job, cleaning, because nobody can say you're not a grafter, but you couldn't cope with being away from Sam, so you phoned her and wrote her every day, but an hour is like a week without her, and you started to sink, which is why you popped on the wing a few times, and they gave you medication [20mg of a fluoxetine anti-depressant]. That's probably not helping with the sleeplessness. You're still gnashing your teeth from it now, like you're on pills [that's your diagnosis, but the gnashing could be caused by stress]. Anyway, you talked to someone [on June 22] and told them about all of this, but they said they couldn't comment on the legal side of things and you should take it up with your solicitor, so you got frustrated and raised your voice, fair enough, saying you had no life to look forward to, because once you got out everything was gone, and you ended up reading the Bible and talking to the chaplain, because you've always been a bit religious. True, you lost your faith over a lot of years, but it's back now, and you definitely believe in the afterlife and God and Jesus, because when you were suffering as a kid you prayed to be massive and all that came true, and while you were inside you prayed to God, and he did give you signs. When people say things like that, about getting signs from God, it's easy to think they're nuts, but it's true. What it was is, since getting this charge, for hitting a kid, everyone had been making you jump through hoops, and you'd been having to go over to the council offices, sitting in these tiny rooms that smelled of curry and farts, like

18

an Indian family had been in there, not being racist or anything, and there were little beasties in the carpet biting everyone, and some little Hitler writing down what you were saying, distorting the truth and turning their paper away if you looked over, like you were copying off the swotty kid at school, and they kept complaining about you being late or missing appointments, even though they knew you were working all over the country, making sure there was something for the future, like, this one time you had to go down south to pick up a car, which is what you do with your vehicle recovery business, so you left Newcastle early in the morning when the weather was terrible, and you assumed the afternoon session would be cancelled, so you didn't show up, but they complained about that and said you should call them next time to check if it's cancelled, but whenever you tried to call, someone else picked up this woman's phone and they'd monkey you around, saying she's on the phone or she's going to ring you back or she can't come to the phone, and you know fine well they were just doing it because they recognised your voice and wanted to mug you off, yet they had no problem with scumbags, people with TVs as big as caravans, gold around their necks, nothing in the cupboards but sausages and beans, no carpets on the floor, they had no problem with them. They just let people like that do as they please, in fact they'd probably rather you were a junkie or a bum, that's the way it seems to work these days, rather than someone like you, who's got none of these flaws, but all you hear is how much of a bad man you are, and they started coming out with tales only a retarded kid could think of, saying you'd threatened them, acting like witches around the coven,

19

treating you like some kind of evil Willie Wonka, and you got shafted and shafted and shafted, and it was all about how Raoul Moat's just a loudmouth arsehole, because you are big, to be fair, and you do get animated, but anyone can be made out to be a monster, the whole tabloid thing. They see how you are in public and think you must be worse when they're not watching you, but that's just you being honest, and what happened is, you started thinking about just leaving the country once you got out, just getting out of jail and going abroad, taking the kids with you, but God sent you this sign. It wasn't a burning bush or walking on water or anything like that, it was just this desperately unhappy little girl. She was in the paper because her dad had taken her abroad and her mum had murdered her. She looked exactly like one of your daughters, and it made you realise that if you took them to live in France they'd be unhappy, just like the little girl in the paper. God was saying it was a bad idea. The next thing that happened, the second sign, came quickly after the first. It was Derrick Bird whacking all those people in Cumbria. He killed twelve of them and disgraced himself really, shooting old ladies with bobble hats and people like that, randomly killing, rather than picking targets, and all he achieved was make people hate him. That was a sign from God that you shouldn't go about blasting random targets. Though something must have pushed him to do it, for this supposedly normal guy to go mad like that, but we don't know what it was, and what you do know is there's nothing wrong with you. You know that for a fact, because when you were seeing the psychiatrist at the Collingwood a few years ago you asked them to check you were on the same page as everyone else, just in case something down the line wasn't right, and they thought you might be paranoid and delusional [a mental health worker referred you to a psychiatrist and suggested you be assessed for psychosis and paranoia], but when they looked into it they discovered you were right, the police do harass you, and it's gone on for years [the psychiatrist said it appeared you were experiencing significant trouble with the police], but there was nothing they could do [you were referred for psychotherapy, but didn't show up], even though it was making you stressed and depressed. They suggested drugs, but you didn't want to start with that, because once you put your hand in the fire it might get burned, and being honest, you are a bit emotionally unstable, you do get over-the-top happy. You have your bad times as well. Like, when someone mocks you or accuses you of something you haven't done you do overreact, which is why this charge and conviction was hard to take. It was all part of the conspiracy, a set-up. It was a ridiculous charge. You were being done for something you didn't do, because if you'd really hit a little kid it would have killed them, which is why you started recording everything, so you could go to the *Chronicle* or on TV, and hit them with everything you had, like you did last time [in 2003 you told the council your daughter fell from your second-floor window and you asked them to put locks on the windows, but you thought it took them too long so you visited their offices], which is when the council accused you of being aggressive and threatening, and you had to tell the reporter it was just anger, but not out of control anger, and all that went in the media, but you didn't go to the media this time. Even so, your whole body language should have told

21

them you never hit a little kid. You were tried, convicted and crucified before you even got to court. Your solicitor said to get your head around the fact that people get booked for things they didn't do, but how can an innocent man accept being hanged? That's why you wanted to do a lie detector test, but your solicitor said no judge would look at it, and the police wouldn't look at it, so you wrote to Jeremy Kyle and asked to go on there and do a lie detector test on TV, because how would they have all felt then? How would they have felt if you'd gone on Jeremy Kyle to do a lie detector, and when he asked if you hit that little kid you turned around and said, *NO, I DIDN'T HIT THAT LITTLE KID*, and the lie detector showed you were telling the truth? How would they have felt then? Because you didn't do any of this. You're the most innocent bloke around, but your best wasn't good enough for them or Sam or the children or yourself. You spent your whole life wanting a family after all these years being alone, and now you've had to watch them slide further and further into the Devil's belly, and you've got nobody to cuddle into, and you miss them so much.

YOU WILL DIE IN SEVEN DAYS

You wake up. You get dressed. You have a shower. It's a bright day again, really summery. You feel strange. Your hair's falling out. You walk across the road to buy milk. You get back and open the laptop. You look at your Facebook status,

Just got out of jail, I've lost everything, my business, my property and to top it all off my lass of six years has gone off with the copper that sent me down. I'm not 21 and I can't rebuild my life. Watch and see what happens.

It's 10.30am. You call Sam. She doesn't answer. You text her. She texts back saying she doesn't have credit to waste. This is what it was like the whole time you were inside, her never answering her phone, her crying whenever she did answer, you trying to make things better by saying you'd be out soon and everything would be okay, but she only came to visit, what, once? That was it, one visit in two months [you were sentenced to four months and served two]. And when she did come you tried to kiss her, but she wouldn't let you, so there was this big shouting match and a scene in the visiting room, and you knew then, because she wasn't being the Sam you knew. Obviously something was going on, while you were stuck inside, in jail, helpless and alone, and finally she did come on the phone, a few weeks before you got out this was, and goes,

It's over, Raoul.

What?

It's over.

What about?

Us.

What for?

Because it is.

Over what?

You know what.

I don't know what.

Without speaking over the phone, you know exactly what, Raoul. I've had enough.

I cannot hear a word you're saying.

I've had enough, Raoul.

Of what?

Everything.

We need to have this conversation later on, because this, this is no good. This is no good at all.

No.

We've had a talk the other day, and you've just started being all micey with me.

No, I haven't.

You have.

You mean we had two arguments the other day?

We had one argument the other day. We had one argument the other day. Let's not get all silly about it, right.

Well no, Raoul, I'm sick.

Well I—

Because I don't want to be with you anymore.

Listen, don't do this when I'm in jail, right.

Well no, I wasn't going to do it in jail, but the, fucking, I don't see why I should wait until you get out, and pretend that everything's fine.

Well no, I know nothing's fine, right, but let's not have this conversation when I'm in jail, right. When I get out I want to talk to you, right.

No, I don't want to talk to you, Raoul. I don't want to see you.

Well what's the problem?

You, you're the problem.

Right, well what's the problem then?

Raoul, you know exactly what the problem is.

I don't know what the problem is.

Oh, what, because we've had such a great relationship, and we've been happy since you went down, have we? Since before you went down, we were happy, were we?

We were having problems, like we're always having problems.

Yes, we were having problems, Raoul, uh-huh.

Because everybody's getting on our case, right, everybody's getting on our case, right, I just want things sorted out in every way, but I can't, I'm struggling, I'm getting fucking sent down, I'm getting harassed, I'm getting picked on, I'm getting all kinds of problems and I cannot do nothing about it.

Raoul, do you know what it is? How do you think I feel? I haven't wanted to be with you since before you got sent down. I'm still sorting fucking loads of shit out for you. I'm still taking fucking dogs to the vets for you, because they're not well. I'm still doing all this shit for you, and I don't want to be with you, Raoul.

Well what's brought this on?

Nothing. This is how I've felt for a long, long time and you know that.

Well no, I haven't known that, because we've never discussed it.

Yeah, and why don't we discuss it? What always happens when I try to leave you? What always happens?

Well no, hang on, you haven't, though, you haven't, though, and I tell you, I tell you what, right, you know while I've been in here, right, this is, this is, it hasn't really come as a bit of a shock, right, but while I've been here and this is something I was wanting to discuss on the way out, there's a lot of kids from your estate, right, I've been getting told a few things, right, so kind of, I have been kind of expecting it because you—

So come on then, what have you been getting told, come on then.

Well I've been told, they've been telling me you've been mucking about.

[She hadn't.]

Oh yeah?

Well no, I have been told that, you know what I mean.

Off who?

And I wanted to see you first, you know, which is exactly why I've just got a letter back today from the GUM clinic saying that everything's okay, which came as a bit of a surprise and I was thinking, right, okay, I'll—

Right, well you know what it is, Raoul, if that's what you fucking think, right, go and fuck yourself. Don't bother ringing my mum, and don't bother ringing me.

Listen, listen, hold on.

Fuck off, no, fuck off.

And she hung up, so obviously you needed a private detective for this kind of operation, someone who could follow her and find out exactly what was going on, which was your dream job when you were a kid to be honest, so you got Karl looking into it, finding a private detective from the phonebook, but when you spoke to Karl on the phone [you made one hundred and eighty-eight phone calls while in prison] he said they were all too expensive, so you told him to just do it and keep an eye on her himself, go through her bins, things like that, but he was useless. Like, she'd tell him how she was at Lightwater Valley or stuck in the house with the puppies, obviously lying [you thought], up to something, but he'd believe it, and he didn't know how to stake her place out either. Like, this one night he parked up to see who was coming and going, and you called him while he was there to make sure he was in the right spot, and even from jail you knew he couldn't see all the exit points, but it's hard to get Karl to understand things like that sometimes, so you told him, if the guy showed up, just do what he needs to do to the guy's car, and Karl asked,

Do you want me to go and get a fiver of petrol or something?

No, no, just key every panel. Don't do nothing like that. Just key every panel. Okay, right, cheers mate. Once she goes to bed I think it's knocking-off time.

The next thing that happens is, a few days before you get out, you call her and say you might be getting released on Thursday, and she says you can't go round there. You were like, what? Why not? And you told her, look, you're not going to cause problems, but she says how she's got an injunction out, so you tell her, look, if she gets all micey then it will go pear-shaped, because

I'm not going to be bullied, Sam. I'm not going to be bullied, right.

And she said,

Raoul, I'm not bullying you. We've split up. We've finished. I don't want you at my house. How is that being bullied?

It was ridiculous. It was hard enough getting your head around it being over, never mind fighting with her as well. Then she says how she's got a new boyfriend, so you told her about knowing that already, and she goes, how could you know, because she's only been seeing him for two days [which was true], and she starts saying how she's not slept with him, and you said, look, hands up, you don't want to fight with her about it, you're not going to bash anyone, but she starts going on about how hard he is. Then she says she doesn't want you to fight him or ruin it, but how could you ruin it, without going AWOL or crackers, which you told her you would if she kept going on like this, but aside from that, how could you possibly ruin it for her? All you wanted was to be able to see her still, not get pushed out, just be able to go round and see her at her house, but she didn't understand why you had to see her if she's got someone new, so you said,

It's not a case of that man, it's just, you know, it hurts not seeing you. You're the only person I've ever cared about like this since the day my gran bloody died, you know what I mean, I cannot have you out of my life, and if you take us, if you take yourself, if you take yourself out of my life, I'm going to go crazy.

Raoul, it's not my fault.

No injunction in the world's going to stop me if you make me go crazy.

And you just kept telling her how you wanted to be able to keep seeing her, and you wouldn't give them problems, but she's saying that you couldn't go to her house or anything, and you said,

Well I can, I can.

And to be honest with you, Raoul, he's a handy fucking bloke anyway, and he isn't going to put up with any shit.

Sam, I don't give a monkey's about that, right.

And he's a lot younger than you.

It doesn't matter, Sam, I'm as handy as they come, right, and I don't care, and you will make a problem between me and him if you push me out.

How can I make a problem between you and him if I push you out? You're my ex and he's my current.

Because, well, it doesn't matter. You'll be nothing if you really, if you really, really hurt me with this, right, I'll end up going for him, and I don't want to.

Well you won't end up going for him, because he'll knock you straight on your fucking arse, Raoul.

He'll not, he'll not.

Yes he will, you'll get a shock.

I'll not.

You will.

Well who is he?

Well I'm not fucking telling you who he is, it's fuck all to do with you.

That's why, well that's what I'm talking about.

But I'm telling you now, he will knock you on your arse.

He'll not.

He fucking will, like.

He'll not, man.

He will.

Well, we'll see, because you've never been scared of anyone. Not that you're violent. Well, you're not a million miles away from being violent, but it's only ever been fisticuffs, giving as good as you get. True, you've got a temper, like, if someone came on to Sam you'd give them a straightener in the toilets. Or if someone's driving dangerously you'd probably try to catch up with them, just to let them know you weren't happy, which is how you broke your hand that time with the guy in the yellow Calibra. Or at home you might lose your temper and break things, or you might hit or slap Sam, or, like, pick her up [and throw her against a door, or drag her downstairs by her hair, or throttle her], but all this stuff about you hitting a little kid, you have never and would never hit a little kid. It's ridiculous, because it would have caused a lot more damage, considering the size of you. You would have killed a little kid by hitting them, but it's all part of the conspiracy.

You call Sam. She doesn't answer.

You call again. She doesn't answer.

You call again. She answers and you argue. She hangs up.

You call again. She doesn't answer.

You call again, again, again.

After lunchtime she texts you. She asks what time Karl's going over to Birtley to collect the puppies. The thing is, the bitch had puppies while you were inside, and Sam's been looking after them, so she wants Karl to go and pick them up and take them to your house, because she's got your daughter at her place and says she doesn't have time to be feeding the puppies every two hours, so you told her you just need to go to B&Q to get some wire mesh, and anyway, it's you who should be pissed off, because nobody said the vet bills were so much, even though you'd warned her that there'd be hell on if you got out and there was no money left, but yes, Karl will get the puppies once you get the wire mesh for your garden to keep them away from the big dogs, one of which is a cross between a Ridgeback and a Staffordshire, and it's so strong its whole body wiggles when it wags its tail.

Karl comes over in the recovery truck and takes you to B&Q in Newburn [in the West End] where you buy a four-man tent [and where you're filmed on CCTV cameras walking round in a fluorescent orange T-shirt]. He drops you at home. You call Sam [at 5.44pm] and she shouts about the puppies again. You tell her to calm down, saying you will get them, but she says Karl has to pick them up now, right now, before tonight, because she wants to go out with her new boyfriend. This is someone she's been seeing for five minutes. Anyway, she says

36

she can't leave the puppies alone, and the conversation goes on like this for half an hour, so fair enough, you're furious by the end of it, because what she's saying is this guy's a police officer, after everything they did to you, after they took everything off you, she's saying he's a copper, and apparently he's going to use the police to get you, so you say to her, look, you want a straightener with this guy. She hangs up.

You call Sam. She doesn't answer.

You text Sam. She doesn't answer.

It's the evening. Karl drives you to KFC. He eats, but you can't. He drives you to Anth's garage in Byker and leaves you there. You chat to Anth and he takes you to KFC. You still can't eat. He says you look ill. You feel like there isn't anybody there, in the place where you're supposed to be. He asks you questions and you try to respond, but there's nothing. He buys you an ice cream, but you don't touch it. You tell him you're not well.

Anth takes you home. You talk for another fifteen minutes in the car. You tell him you'll see him tomorrow in town for a good night out. You tell him you'll get down the gym this week too. You ask if he can get you some protein powder. He asks again if you're okay. You tell him you feel better. You say goodbye.

...

You phone Sam's dad and talk about the puppies, and Sam and this other guy and whether he's a karate instructor or a policeman, but her dad doesn't have answers. The call lasts ten minutes.

...

You're in the house when Sam texts [at 9.36pm]. She says she's on a night out, and her dad's just been on to her and told her he's calling the RSPCA because the puppies shouldn't be left outside tonight. She texts again [at 9.55pm], saying thanks for spoiling her night out and her mum and dad are arguing because of the puppies. You call her again and again. No answer. At 11pm you get in the van with the gun. Karl drives you down the A1 to Birtley, the same journey as last night, same gun as last night.

At 11.07pm you call Sam.

You call her again at 11.13pm.

Again at 11.19pm.

At 11.24pm she picks up. You talk for a few minutes. She's gone again. You sit in the van. You're parked in a car park near her house, round the back of the pub. Your phone battery runs out and you get furious, because she's out somewhere with this guy and you don't know where she is and you can't even call her, so Karl drives you home and you find another battery and

38

get back in the van. You bang the door shut and yell, because she has no idea how this feels, to be this helpless, and you call her again [at 11.47pm]. You call seventeen times and leave one text message. At 11.55pm she answers. You argue. She hangs up. You call again. You get through and her mum [who lives a few doors down from Sam] starts going on, and Jackie takes the phone and starts going on too [she's Sam's friend and neighbour]. Apparently they're all at Jackie's house. You bang the dashboard and yell again. Karl drives you across the river to Birtley. He parks near Sam's house. You say goodbye and he says all the best. You get out the van with the shotgun. You walk to Jackie's. You creep through the garden, quietly. You sneak up to the window, silently. You crouch under the large bay window. One pane is open. They're smoking. You can smell the smoke drifting out. You can hear Sam in there. You hear her talking. You can hear him talking. You hear Jackie. You hear Jackie's husband and Sam's mum. They're all laughing and drinking. It's 1am. The air is warm. You have the bag of cartridges and the shotgun. Karl texts you,

We'll all miss you mate if it goes down.

You text back,

No problem mate, you're the best.

You text Karl again, telling him they're all slagging you off and it's hard to hear this coming from Sam, after all you've been through together. She's like a different person. You text Karl,

39

telling him it sounds like your suffering is funny to them. You tell him you're not happy. You might try to get through the window. Does he think you should try it? He doesn't reply.

You text him again,

I'm going to kick nice and proper when they are out. Then we'll see who's laughing.

You wait.

You wait.

You hear them leaving [at 2.40am]. The front door opens. Sam and him come out. They're holding hands, giggling. They walk out the front gate and onto the pavement. You stand up. You load two cartridges into the gun. They see you. He stands in front of Sam. He stands in front of Sam. He's big, but he's not as big as you.

You raise the gun.

You shoot him in the chest.

…

You just shot him in the chest.

…

...

[You shot him in the heart and liver.]

...

He stays on his feet. He stumbles a few yards, and a bit further, onto the grass, in front of the houses, onto the big grassy bit where it's bright from the streetlights. Sam follows him.

She follows him.

She looks at you. You point the gun at her legs. She turns and runs back into the house. Her mum shouts from somewhere,

You shot him, you bastard.

You hear her, but you don't see her. You look at Sam's new boyfriend. He's running away. You lift the gun and shoot him again, further away though, and it hits him in the neck and he goes down, onto the grass, onto his hands and knees. You loved Sam and if someone takes away someone you love it probably does make you want to kill them. It's a pet hate of yours. You walk over to him. He's on his hands and knees. You stand inches from him. You stand over him. You remove the two spent cartridges. You put new cartridges in, but one falls to the ground. You try again and it goes in this time. You point the gun at his head. Inches away. You shoot him in the head.

41

...

He falls flat.

...

This feels okay.

...

He's lying on the grass. He's dead.

...

You turn around and look at the house, but everyone's gone, every man for himself, except Sam, brave Sam, who's inside, standing at the lounge window, watching, looking at you as you point the gun at her and shoot her through the window.

...

She goes down.

...

Through her arm and into her abdomen.

...

Her dad is standing outside his house, a few doors down. You see him. He makes eye contact with you. He's trying to work out what's happening. Someone shouts,

He's got a gun. Get an ambulance.

You run down the cut between the houses, towards the van. The van is gone. Karl has gone. How can you get home? You run.

It's a warm night. You keep going in the dark.

You see a phone box. You call Anth on your mobile. He picks up. You tell him you've done it. You hang up and call him from the phone box. He answers. You tell him you've done it and the police are trying to kill you.

He asks what you're talking about,

What've you done?

I've done them.

You tell him you were outside the window listening to them slag you off and you've done them. You've done them. He asks what you're on about and you tell him he's gone, Sam's boyfriend is gone. He asks if you shot him. He's gone. You put three in him.

He asks,

How do you know he's dead?

Listen, Anth, he's gone.

He asks about Sam. You tell him she's okay, she crawled away, and finally he's getting the gist of it. You tell him you're sorry for the time you fell out, but you've got to get off, the police are trying to kill you. He asks what you'll do. You tell him you're going to kill yourself, or take on the police. You tell him,

I love you, mate.

You put the phone down and keep running to Chester-le-Street and get to the taxi rank and take off your hoodie and roll it around the gun and flag down a taxi and get in, which is a struggle, because you're big, and you tell the taxidriver you want to go to Newburn [near Tara's house, in the West End]. He drives onto the A1, over the river, and as he drives he tries to make conversation, but you cut him off, blanking him, avoiding eye contact in the mirror. He gets to Newburn and asks,

Where to now?

You tell him to pull off the A1 at the next junction and go a bit further, stop here. You don't ask how much it is, just hand him a £20 note, which isn't enough, but he takes it and says nothing. You step out with the gun tucked tight so he can't see it and you walk to Shipley Street, to Tara's house. Karl and Sean show up. The three of you stand in the kitchen. You tell

44

them you feel like a great weight has been lifted. You tell Sean to ring 118 118 for your solicitor. He dials and says the name of your solicitor, but the operator can't find it, and you tell Sean to hang up because they can't use their phones anymore. You give them £200 and tell them to go to Tesco's to buy some pay-as-you-go phones. You wait in the house, and this doesn't feel real anymore. It takes them an hour. When they get back you tell Sean you're taxing his Lexus and he can be the driver, and Karl gets in the passenger seat. You get in the back with the gun. Sean drives to Byker, where Karl left the van with the tent in the back of it, so Sean gets out and gets the tent out the van and puts it in the Lexus. Sean drives again. You tell him to head to Rothbury, giving him directions as he drives, six or seven miles past Morpeth, then a left, and carry on for about ten miles out into the sticks, where the houses are cheap because they get snowed in during winter, and there's nothing to do, but you can choose your own Christmas trees out here, and this is where you and Sam were looking at getting a place, near Rothbury somewhere, a house out by itself with a bit of land, like when you were in France with your dad, who's a French farmer, that whole side of the family are French farmers, down by the border with Spain, and you spent a lot of your time down there with your dad as a kid, among the cottages and vineyards, you've got these happy memories of it, so yeah, it would have been ideal, for you and Sam to have lived out here, the kids would have loved it, somewhere different, somewhere nice, that was their dream.

You get to Rothbury at 6am. It's light already. You tell Sean to pull into a little car park by some industrial units, and you all get out and carry the tent along a track, through a hedge, to the corner of a field, sheltered by trees and bushes, and you say,

We can chill out over here.

It takes fifteen minutes to put the tent up, and the sky is bright and the birds are chirping, and it's peaceful, and you're feeling better than you've felt in months, full of beans.

YOU WILL DIE IN SIX DAYS

It's 7am. Karl and Sean go shopping. You stay at the tent. You're grinding your teeth. Your jaw is aching. You punch your legs.

...

Obviously you're not going to be around in a few days.

...

It feels strange.

...

You walk down the track. There's a woman on a horse, fucking hell, so you crouch down and pretend to tie your shoes, and you keep your face hidden, and walk onto the grass verge, and she's gone.

...

This is easy.

...

Karl and Sean get back. You ask if they were followed. They say they weren't. They've got bags of stuff:

pillows, sleeping bags, duvet

white baps, sausages, premium burgers

water

shower gel, toothbrushes, toothpaste, toilet roll, disposable razors

portable barbecue, barbecue tools, charcoal, lighter fluid

bowls, washing-up liquid, bin bags, tin opener

notebook, biros, envelopes

a bottle of Reggae Reggae Sauce.

Karl lights the barbie, and the three of you eat. After a few burgers, Karl and Sean write their letters — one from Karl to his sister-in-law, who lives with Karl's brother, telling her she shouldn't be alarmed, but you're holding him hostage and treating him like a gent, and you're a nice bloke, you've just got your problems, don't we all, and you're a mate so he's going to do what he can to help you, and she should tell his mum what's happening, but not let her go to the police because then he won't be coming back. Signed Karl. You read it after he's finished.

Sean writes a letter to his sister saying he's being held hostage by a man with a shotgun, but you're treating him well and buying him what he needs. He also writes another letter to her,

BURN THIS LETTER!!!

IT IS MY FRIEND THAT IS HOLDING ME 'HOSTAGE' I AM ACTUALLY SAFER THAN SAFE. BUT THIS DEED WILL SEE ME A MADE MAN. IM ACTUALLY HIDDEN OUT AT A SECRET LOCATION WELL OUT OF HARMS WAY. BURN THIS LETTER AFTER YOU HAVE READ IT, NOT SURE ABOUT SHOWING IT TO MAM & DAD THOUGH AS THEY WILL SPILL THE BEANS AND THAT WILL LEAD ME TO ACTUALLY BEING SHOT. LOVE YOU!!! XXX

You read his letters too. Karl has a kip in the tent. You tell Sean to get himself to Smokey Joe's in town [Newcastle] and buy a portable TV to keep track of the news. He heads to the car.

You chill out.

...

At 4.05pm Sean texts,

won't get tv anywhere not even smokey joes

Fucking hell. You call him. Then he calls you and says he can't find the other shop you told him to try, but he's got clothes from Primark, and he texts again,

in asda, got fm radio

He's back at base camp by teatime, and you ask if he was followed, and he says he wasn't. He's brought ice creams. You eat the ice creams, and Karl cooks more sausages, and you sit by the barbecue talking about how good the sausages smell. A man comes through the hedge and asks if the track goes any further. Sean tells him it doesn't, and he goes away. It gets dark. You've got a plan.

...

You all get in the car.

...

Sean drives. You tell him to stop at the garage to grab the paper. He gets out and gets the paper and comes back and passes it to you. You read in the back seat.

...

Sean drives.

...

It says Sam's in critical condition. Your head's a mess right now, and you're probably too far gone to make sense of it, but you're definitely sorry about shooting her. You didn't mean to do that, not make her critical, but being honest, you meant to do what you meant to do, and you're thinking, if all the things that have happened to you had happened to someone else, would it have gone this far? Probably not. You've got issues. No doubt about that. Obviously this isn't normal. Normal people don't do things like this. But you've got a funny frame of mind at the minute. Being honest, the only emotion you actually feel is how you feel about Sam, but it's clouded by something else, something you don't understand: you don't actually feel anything. It's like you could just go out and buy an ice cream and go to the cinema like nothing's wrong. Strange. Your doctor said years ago that if someone in your family is a manic, or maniac, or something like that, whether it just makes you, you know, not understand what you're doing. You can guarantee there's probably a chemical being released somewhere in your body that isn't right, because you do get hyperactive and don't sleep and can't sit still. You've got to be up doing something all the time. It's unusual. Jail made it worse. While you were inside you had these thoughts about blowing up Etal Lane police station, because you do have explosives knowledge and you've got access to chemicals, so it's something you could do, and you're still thinking about doing it, and you've been wondering

53

about it for three years, because that place has been a cause of so many of your problems. Like, they bully you. A lot of people think the police can't bully someone like you, but they do, and the thing that always stopped you retaliating is you're fucked once you do something like that. That's it, your life's over. You flush your life down the toilet as soon as you do anything like that, which is why you always put it on a backburner. Because you lose everything then. That's why nobody in the history of mankind has taken the police on before. No one's been daft enough, except you, but you were really hurt this time. You were wanting to do things you wouldn't normally want to do. You thought about hurting Sam, doing a bit more than hurting her, and you broke down, because it's not what you wanted. It's not what you wanted at all. You shouldn't be thinking like that, but this is what happens when that side of you takes over. It upsets you, and it's happened for years, but nobody ever tried to help you with it. Nobody ever turned around and said, look, Raoul, you've got this problem. The amount of times you've gone to shrinks and said, look, is it me, analyse me, fix me, whatever's wrong, fix it, but not one's come back and said there's something wrong. Well, sorry, but you beg to fucking differ. You might not have a degree, but when most people get bullied they just take their own life, still bound by the rules, but not you, you go chasing other people. Fucking Joe Soap down the road isn't sitting here planning how to kill a police officer, is he?

...

Sean stops the car outside Karl's sister-in-law's in Dudley. Karl gets out and goes to the front door. He comes back after a few minutes and says he gave the letter to her dad.

...

Sean drives to Blyth. You drop the letters off.

...

He drives to Scott's house [who got the van for Karl]. Karl goes to the door and leaves the key for the van so he can get rid of it.

...

Sean drives to Andy's house in Newcastle [a friend]. He gives you a phone, but the SIM isn't registered.

...

You tell Sean to drive to your house. The police are outside, swarms of them, looking for you. You tell Sean to drive, onto the West Road. He stops at a garage for a SIM card and chocolate bars. It's after midnight. He gets back in and drives west.

The SIM works. You dial 999. They answer. You say,

Hello there, this is the gunman from Birtley last night. My name is Raoul Moat. What I'm phoning about is to tell you exactly why I've done what I've done, right. Now my girlfriend has been having an affair behind my back with one of your officers, this gentleman that I shot last night, the karate instructor, right. Now you bastards have been on to me, right, for years. You've hassled me, harassed me, you just won't leave me alone. I went straight six years ago when I met her and I have tried my best to have a normal life and you just won't let up, right. You won't leave me alone for five minutes. I can't drive down the street without the blue flashing lights, you know. You've stitched me up for years. You've been caught stitching me up. So the fact of the matter is, right, she's had an affair with one of your officers.

Yep.

If he had not been a police officer I would not have shot him.

Okay.

It's as simple as that, right. But the thing is, you know, it's been going on for a while. I went to jail, right.

Right, right.

I went to jail for something I didn't do. Now I could have took a community order, right, but what happened is me and Sam had a discussion with me barrister, that if I went to jail, within three to four weeks me barrister promised us, and they let us down, she said she would have us on a retrial, get the not guilty so me and my Sam could live together. Now I've went to jail, right—

56

Slow down a minute, because you're losing me there.

Right.

Uh-huh.

Well I went to jail longer than I should have done for something I didn't do, right. Which, justify that in your own head, right.

Yes.

And meanwhile, while I'm doing that for my missus, she's having an affair with one of your officers, right, and then when I come out, right, she's winding us up, saying that you are going to stitch us up, using him.

Yeah.

Right, and you know that he's this, he's that, he's going to, because he's a multiple black belt, he's going to kick me arse all over the place, you know what I mean.

Right, okay, okay, mm-hm.

And I've had nothing but grief, and I've had a good relationship with her for six years, which is why we've stayed together. I've gone straight. I've had a totally legitimate life with her. I've opened a business. And I have been shafted, and you police have took too much off me over the years.

Okay.

You won't leave us alone, and now you think you can take my missus. Now I didn't mean to shoot her like that, right, that was—

Okay, okay.

He deserved it, right, but she, right, you can see from the ballistics, I've been altering those cartridges, right. That one was only half the powder. It was only meant to get her compensation, because obviously I'm not going to be around in a few days, right, it was meant to just give her a little injury so she can get loads of compensation.

Okay.

Now that I've found out she's critical I'm not happy about it. I didn't mean that, you know what I mean.

Right, right.

I can't, I can't, to be honest with you, I'm quite surprised she is critical, you know, but I didn't mean that, but the fact of the matter is I'm not coming in alive. You've hassled me for so many years. If you come anywhere near me I'll kill you. I've got two hostages at the minute, right. Come anywhere near me and I'll kill them as well. I'm coming to get you. I'm not on the run. I am coming to get you. You've made me unwell. You've made me do this because you just won't leave me out, you know, you just won't leave me alone.

Can you confirm you've got two hostages?

I confirm I've got two hostages, yes.

Right, and, and where are you?

I'm not going to tell you where I am.

Okay, fair enough, yep.

I'm coming to get you, don't worry, right.

Can I just confirm who you are? Can you give me your date of birth please?

Yes, it's the seventeenth of June 1973.

Right, okay then, thank you very much.

Right. I am very sorry for what's happened with Sam, that's not what I meant, you know ...

As you talk on the phone you're telling them how Sam's changed, she hasn't half changed, and Sean's driving over a roundabout with a T5 [a police car] parked on it, a police officer inside, waiting to bully someone, probably a single mum who couldn't afford to pay her car tax, and the person on the phone's saying,

59

Right, right.

She wouldn't let me go up to her house. She wouldn't discuss anything. And she was threatening me with one of your officers, right. Now I've had enough. I've had enough of you. That jail made me unwell. I came out a different kid, you know what I mean. I've lost everything through you, right. You just won't leave me alone, right. So at the end of the day, you killed me. You killed me and him, before that trigger was ever pulled.

Right.

You know what I mean.

Okay.

You've pushed me.

We are trying to help you, yep.

You're not trying to help me, you're not trying. You wanted me to do myself in and I was going to do it until I found out about him properly, and what was going on, and as soon as I found out he was one of your officers I thought, nah, you've had too much from me, you've had too much from me. You'll get your chance to kill me, right, you'll get your chance to kill me.

We don't want to do that. We don't want to do that.

Yes, you do. You wanted me to kill myself, but I'm going to give you a chance, because I am hunting for officers now, right.

No. Please don't do that. We don't want any more killing, alright?

You hang up. Karl dismantles the phone. He puts the pieces in a bag. You're on the A69. Sean pulls over. Karl puts the bag under a road sign. He gets back in, and Sean turns the car around.

...

He drives back to the roundabout, past the T5 again. He drives down onto the A1, to the next junction. He pulls off the A1 and turns back around, along the A1 again, to the slip road leading up to the roundabout with the T5 parked on it.

You tell him to drive slowly. Turn the lights off.

He puts the blinkers on. You tell him to turn them off.

He stops the car on the slip road.

You tell him to stay here.

You get out and stay low, crouched behind the concrete barrier, creeping up behind the T5, a few long strides, to the passenger window, stand up quickly, you can see the officer's legs, he's on the driver's side, he leans over, looks at your face, he sees the butt of the gun against your chest, he sees your right finger on the trigger, and your left hand holding the barrel.

He looks at the gun.

...

He looks in your left eye.

...

You pull the trigger.

...

The flash comes out like a cone.

There's blood.

Face. Fluid

Spray

His eye has gone.

...

He goes down. Slumped.

...

You fire again.

...

At the back of his head, at his left upper body.

He doesn't move.

...

There are two small holes in the window.

You run back to your car.

...

You dive in and shout,

Fast, fast, fast, fucking drive!

Or

Go, go, go!

It's hard to know, because everything happens so quick. Sean puts the pedal to the metal, the doors still open, tyres screeching, over the roundabout, down the slip road, tooling it up the A1. You sit in the back and unfold the shotgun. Two used cartridges come out. The car smells of spent cartridges.

I don't think he's dead.

That's what you tell them.

You say he went down with the first shot, but the second shot, all you could see was the back of his head, so you shot him there.

They'll all be shitting themselves now.

Ha ha

…

[Lacerations. Soft-tissue damage. Puncture wounds. Broken bones.]

…

You reload and tell Sean to spin round.

You want to see what's happening. He drives to your house. All the police have gone.

He keeps driving, towards the roundabout, where the T5 was, but there's a roadblock, so he turns off.

The police are running round like mice.

You drive past a man in a high-vis vest. He's got an Alsatian with him, walking in the long grass. You could shoot him too.

But you don't.

Sean keeps driving.

Onto the A69, where you left the phone. Karl gets out, picks the phone up, gets in the car, puts it back together. It's 1.39am.

You call 999,

Hello, this is Raoul, the Birtley gunman. Are you taking me serious now? Are you taking me seriously?

Sorry?

Are you taking me serious now? I've just downed your officer at the roundabout at the West End of Newcastle.

Yes.

Yeah, well, I'm going to destroy a few lives like you've destroyed mine. Sam and the bairn were everything I held personal and everything meant in the world to me, and you've even taken that. You couldn't just leave me with her. You've taken that as well. I've got no life left. There's nothing for me to play with. This is what happens, this is what happens when you push, push, push and push, you know, you've left me nothing to play with now. Are you proud of yourselves, you know? Does this make you happy now? People are getting hurt now.

Hello?

Can you hear?

I can, yes, I thought you'd gone off-air.

No, I hadn't gone off.

Where are you? Are you—

I'm not going to tell you. Listen, I'm going to keep coming for you. I'm not going to stop, like you didn't stop for me, right. This is how far you've pushed me. There's no need for it. I've lost everything. I'm really sorry that I've hurt my Sam. I didn't mean to hurt her like that. I just meant her to get compensation and be set for life without me. But you, I do mean to hurt. You've not left me alone for years. You couldn't just leave me with her, could you?

Right, okay then, but, erm, which way—

That's what I'm telling you now. I'm absolutely not going to stop.

You're not—

You're going to have to kill me. But I'm never going to stop.

You hang up.

Karl dismantles the phone and leaves it on a grass verge.

...

Sean drives back to base camp.

...

Karl sleeps. You can't sleep. Sean can't sleep either.

The two of you sit up and talk.

He asks about the thing on the A69. He wants to know how it felt, so you tell him, how the hairs on the back of your neck would normally prickle when you saw a T5, because you'd be thinking, here we go again, expecting to get pulled, and sure enough you'd get pulled, but this time you just remedied the problem, and he's never going to pull you again. It felt easy, being honest. Just casually walking up and getting the job done. You felt nothing, not at the time. You feel much better now though. You've declared war on Northumbria Police. Good. You're not daft, you know it's not a war you can win, but it's about time people knew the police aren't perfect, that some of the worst kids from school became police officers. People should know the truth about them. And the fact that

67

Northumbria Police are finally taking you seriously, it doesn't make you feel big or clever, but it does give a bit of satisfaction. It's not over though. This is just the beginning.

You tell Sean you want to shoot a social worker.

You have a good chat about it.

YOU WILL DIE IN FIVE DAYS

Today's a chill-out day. Kind of a day off.

Karl and Sean have a lie in while you write an eight-page letter to Sam. You write her a 'Get Well Soon' card as well. You wish you could have visited her in hospital, but it's impossible, thanks to the police, so you're sending her a card instead. The front's got a poorly monkey on it with a thermometer in its mouth.

It says,

You're in hospital … but luckily the doctors say you'll be normal in no time!

Then inside it says,

Well, that'll be a first.

You write beneath that,

71

No joke intended. Get well soon, Raoul.

...

Karl and Sean get up. It's the afternoon.

Karl puts the barbie on and cooks burgers and sausages.

You listen to the radio.

You read the Sunday papers.

...

Your face is on the front of most of them, but it's all lies, and the way you see it is, the public deserves to know the truth, so you sit in the tent with a notepad and pen, and you write your murder statement [this is an edited and rewritten version of your full statement; the full statement was forty-nine pages long and included accusations, odd logic and incoherent explanation; the following are your thoughts rather than facts],

RAOUL MOAT MURDER STATEMENT 4/7/10

On the night 3/7/10 I shot Chris Brown and Samantha Stobbart after an argument earlier that evening. Here I will make all facts clear so there is no misunderstanding about the events which took place and the build-up to these events. Sam used to go to Newcastle city to drink and she'd talk to me while

72

I was working on the door of Liquid Bar in the Bigg Market. She was in a relationship with someone else though, so I stated nothing could happen while she was with him because there are enough women in the world not to mess around with someone else's, and I take a dim view of those who do, which is why I have a history of violence over ex-partners' bits on the side, though much of this is exaggerated. What I didn't want was Sam to be sneaking around, which would in effect cheapen her, so I made my feelings clear. Even kissing would have been a poor start. I just wanted the whole package to keep because I loved her right from the start and she claimed the same. After a few months nothing changed though, so I stated that she had two weeks to finish with him. That time passed and nothing happened, so I started seeing another girl I'd been out with a few times previous, who was a bit big for my taste really, but soon after that Sam stated she'd left him. Hands up here, later that week I found out she was only 16. This made me nervous as she could hurt me emotionally, being so young. I'd only had one young girlfriend previous and that relationship had failed, but on New Year's Eve I met up with Sam at Liquid and she made her feelings clear. We had a good talk and started our relationship. She quickly packed in her job and I was working on the doors at that time so we spent all day, every day together. We grew closer and I never left her side. She was like no other. She changed my view on life, being honest. All my adult life I've felt alone, estranged from my entire family, needing to belong, but I never did. I used to fill the gap with beautiful women, but all the relationships failed and it was never enough, no matter how good the looks and personality. Other blokes would have given an arm for what I had, but I was never happy, and that frame of mind is contagious, it can drag partners down with you. Coming to Marissa, I was seeing her from 1998 to 2003 [a different date than you gave at other times] and we had two kids together, but we were always arguing and had serious fights. Sometimes the police got involved. I freely admit I hit her, but 90% of the stuff I was being arrested for was rubbish. The police bullied me, seeing a big guy as a target. I'd argue back and seal my own fate. I had 184 traffic stops in 2005 and not much less in 2006 [Northumbria Police recorded you being stopped fourteen times between 2000 and 2010]. Looking at my arrests [you were arrested twelve times and found guilty once] people can draw one conclusion. I'll hold my hands up and admit I was a bad lad at one time, but the arrests are the untrue side. Most of what I've done I've gotten away with and the crimes I committed were only against people who wronged me. No innocent member of the public is unsafe, let's be clear about that. But it was a witch-hunt, and it goes back years, when I was on the doors and this woman tried to get friendly with me, bringing me odd gifts and things like that. Someone said she was involved with the police. Well, I'm no Columbo, but I decided to prove it by telling her this story I made up about this other guy getting my girlfriend at the time pregnant. I told her I was going to invite this guy fishing and push him off a cliff, you know, have himself a fall. I arranged for it to happen that weekend. Anyway, it worked like a dream, because the police got involved immediately, which to me basically blew her cover [or showed that someone who had heard about your plan told the police], and I'm almost certain nobody else told the police, but anyway, that night the woman called me a loner, saying how I was born with nothing, and the police would see to it that I never had anything [you later said she didn't actually mention the police], which I pooh-poohed at the time, but now I understand how powerful they are. Like the visit from the Environment Agency about fly-tipping. What was all that about? And cars getting uplifted. But this is just a taste of what's gone on. Coming back to Sam. The first 6 months were fantastic. It was clear she was the one. Even when her family fell out with me she chose to stay with me. This was a massive wake-up call. Never had anyone devoted themselves to me like this. It was my turning point. All my life I'd wanted death, hence the risks and making the worst kind of enemies. I was shot at 3 times, but didn't care. Now I wanted life and I wanted it with my Sam. She helped me be who I really wanted to be. She was beautiful and sexy and the best company ever. We made it special and she was perfect. She was possessive and jealous, which I liked at times. I told her there was nothing to fear, but what stressed her was me and Marissa staying in touch. This caused arguments. I didn't understand at the time, but now I do, and one day I pushed Sam. She fell and cut her head. I was really sorry. It came out of nowhere. She was upset. I was upset. I didn't think I could do that to her. Once I was calm I told her violence only gets worse and I didn't want that with her, so I said next time I'd leave, and I began to remove Marissa from my life. I now know that jealousy is just another form of love. It meant that Sam really loved me. Over time our relationship grew stronger, but one thing bothered me, my age. Yes, good stuff was happening and I was changing into a better and more normal person. I realised my whole life had been a mistake and packed in the door work to please Sam. The bodybuilding wasn't so important as it was mainly a protection thing anyway, and for the first time I was with a woman and not thinking about anyone else. I'd fallen in love, like in the books. I worshipped the ground she walked on and I couldn't be far from her. I wanted to be with her forever, but there was that niggling problem, that sooner or later I would get old on her and she might want to leave. She might resent it. What a kick in the teeth, to be shown life in the arse end of my youth. To be giving me Sam, the one, at an age when I could lose her. If I lost her I knew I'd go back to my old ways. I tried to stop thinking about it. That life before her was awful in so many ways, so the best way to keep her was to be the best I could be. But with every day I grew older. Every day I worried more. She stayed though. We had a few small time-outs in the first year, mostly because of insecurities about my devotion, but she knew that shock tactics got my attention and made me give her whatever she wanted to persuade her to come back. Anyway, my child with Sam was born, sealing my dedication to Sam. I enjoyed watching Sam grow as she became the mother of my daughter. We planted bulbs one summer's day and I'll never forget it. I sat for a minute and stared at her while she continued planting them, the most beautiful woman in the world, right there, with me, doing something really ordinary. It was a perfect moment. Mad as it sounds, it doesn't get better than being there and feeling what I felt in that garden. I just wished I'd been her age, that I'd met her at school and married her straight away instead of wasting my life. But it was like God had cut me a

76

break and sent her from the heavens to guide me. The more I loved, the more I wanted to give back, so I started this gardening business, Mr Trimmit, to secure our future. I worked hard, 7 days a week, sometimes late, and me and Sam didn't see much of each other. We missed each other. I'd get back and she'd be in the garden. Every day had this perfect moment. But I missed them so much. My life was clean and honest. I loved it, except being away all day. What I didn't realise was I was drifting away from Sam because of that time apart. I didn't see it until there were problems. The thing is, Sam was young and she was missing me so much. I'd come in, tired, and we'd argue. On occasions there'd be a bit of pushing and shoving, which upset us both. On a few occasions it went a bit further because Sam would say something very hurtful which would cut deep, but I never punched her. I slapped her and grabbed her or pushed her. To try and fix things I started working less hours. It went well again, and Sam loved me more than ever, but she didn't know if she could carry on. Perfection was going wrong. I thought about giving up Mr Trimmit, but I never wanted Sam to put her hand in her pocket and just feel her leg. It would have been a waste. So I carried on, but on the 13th of January 2009 Sam left. I was devastated. I didn't know where she had gone. Eventually I tracked her down at her gran's house and had many discussions with her about what to do. She agreed to see me on Valentine's Day, but wouldn't let me book a hotel. We had a nice time in the house. All the cards came on the table and I wanted to have sex, or should I say making love as it would have been, but she stopped it. I carried on seeing her daily and doing my duty with the kids, but it drained me emotionally. I was crying a lot. Doing my duties was so difficult. In June the allegation came [about hitting a child]. Full details can be obtained from my solicitor. Every day I told Sam I loved her. I told her I'd never strayed while we were apart. She never seemed convinced, but honestly, if another woman came over I wanted to punch them straight away. No other woman would ever compare. It was back to like it was at the beginning for a few months. Sam went to live at her mum's over winter. I saw her still, but this charge was hanging over me. Sam ended up crying most days. These were hard times emotionally. Then she took a house a few doors away from her mum's. And when I appeared in court these idiots found me guilty. Sam seemed to give up on our relationship. The month before sentencing was upsetting as she seemed distant. I tried to connect without success and she started spending a lot of time elsewhere. One night I demanded the truth, wanting to know if there was someone else. She cried a lot and said there wasn't [there wasn't]. She just wanted to talk about the kids, which I saw as another sign of cheating [she wasn't]. On the day of sentencing I rejected the Community Order and agreed to go to jail so I'd get a quicker retrial, so there wouldn't be any complications about me living with Sam. I love Sam more than anything. But I underestimated how hard jail would be. It's proper shit. I couldn't hack being away from Sam. Time has no meaning in jail. Then these rumours reached me [which were false]. It was unbearable. Sam ended it and that finished me off. They gave me medication. Days before being released she said she had someone else. Once I got out I decided to end my life with a shotgun I obtained, but after the first night I promised to give it one last try with Sam. Unfortunately on the night of the shooting she goaded me. I told her I was at her house and I was prepared to fight Chris because I was sick of the threats. I wanted to show him up. She stated it would be too severe a fight because we're both large and heavily trained in martial arts, and she said she'd talk to me tomorrow. Then my battery ran out. I went home for the charger, rang her, and we argued again. It was unbelievable. She even denied the conversation about getting a quick retrial had taken place [one of several conversations you appear to have misunderstood], so I went bonkers and told her I wanted a fight. Then her mum started in with her childish mouth, saying to get over it, and her neighbour, Jackie, started too, before she hung up. I forced Karl Ness to drive me over to Jackie's house and wait for me to shoot Chris. I hid under the window for an hour and a half, listening to them mocking me. It was hurtful. If I was ever going to back down, hearing them saying those things stopped that. Sam was all I cared about in the world. I didn't want to live without her. She couldn't be replaced, and he was the reason we were apart. So if I'm off, then so is he. I warned them, but they wouldn't listen. The police had taken everything. Now they wanted my all-time love. Had he been an ordinary guy and not police I wouldn't have shot him. At 2.30am they came out. I shot him in the chest and he ran off. I fired a second shot and he went down. I pointed at Sam to chase her and she ran off. Her mum was screaming. I reloaded two customised rounds. One for Sam and one for him. Sam's was half the powder with small gauge pellets. With a superficial injury, she would get a massive compensation payout for her and the kids' future, inadvertently providing for them when I'm gone. There would be small scarring reminding her not to do this to anyone again. How could she have done this to me? I read in the paper about Sam's gran saying I bruised Sam, but I never bruised her. Ever. Stick that lying cunt on a lie detector [you admitted that you hit Sam]. As for these other claims, they'll be paid witnesses. Fucking lying cunts. I've a good mind to come back and shoot them. Anyway, I put the third round in his head and went to the window and fired at Sam. It hit. She seemed okay, but I paused to be sure. She crawled to the kitchen and hid behind the door. Her mum had fucked off upstairs. Typical. [She went upstairs before Sam was shot to hide the children.] I went to shoot myself then changed my mind because I'm determined to get the police back. Karl had gone so I made my way to Chester-le-Street and got a taxi after phoning Anth Wright. I took two hostages and went to ground. Last night I declared war on Northumbria Police before shooting an officer. They're going to pay for what they've done to me and Sam. The public need not fear me, but the police should because I won't stop until I'm dead. And I never hit that little kid [you were found guilty in court]. I could simply admit to anything now because it doesn't matter. I'm a killer and a maniac, but I'm not a coward. And with Sam, I was terrified of losing Sam, as I knew I'd lose the plot if it happened, so that stopped me from ever beating Sam [again, you admitted you hit her]. Anyone saying otherwise can go on a lie detector. I'm gutted she's really hurt. These doctors had better save her or I'll hit that hospital. I'm still chomping my jaw, like I'm on ecstasy. I thought it was the medication, but I've been off that since I came out. It feels like I'm watching a film, not real at all. I guess I've finally lost it. My hostages are safe and the police know they will only be harmed if I'm raided. I'm not on the run. I will keep killing police until I am dead. They've hunted me for years, now it's my turn to hunt them. I am very sorry about Sam. I wish I hadn't shot her. Just make sure she stays alive. I never cheated on her. I wish she hadn't on me [she didn't], but by doing so she pulled the trigger just as much as me.

You sign your name and print it,

R.T.Moat

...

Karl cooks more burgers. Sean writes another letter to his sister, which you read. He says you're treating him good and will get him a dictaphone so he can interview you, and she shouldn't worry, because you're not out to hurt anybody but the people who bullied and tortured you for years, and she should console his mum and dad if they know, and keep these notes for future reference.

He also writes a letter to his friend, which you read. He says it's no joke, he's being held by the Birtley gunman, and please ring his sister to tell her he's okay, and the rent for the lock-up will be late, and nigga hoi the kettle on [a private joke].

Sean starts writing his diary of being a hostage. It's going to be an account of his time with you. He might turn it into a book.

...

Karl writes another letter to his sister-in-law [which she never receives]. You read it. He says you shot a policeman last night, but she shouldn't worry, and he's still a hostage, but is being fed and watered, and you're going to kill as many police as you can before getting gunned down yourself.

...

It's dark. You walk to the car park. Karl and Sean come with you. A guy's moving a branch out the road. It must have blown down.

Sean says something about it being a breezy night, but you and Karl keep your heads down. Another guy is walking his dogs. Nice night, one of you says, then you get in the car. Sean drives.

...

You go to Karl's brother's house to drop off the second letter [it gets dropped through the letterbox; nobody's home].

...

You go to your friend Andy's house in Newcastle, the same one as last night, and hand over the 49-page murder statement you wrote today. You tell him it needs to go to the *Chronicle*.

...

You go to Sean's lock-up in Blaydon. He presses the key fob. Karl goes inside and gets a shotgun. Now you've got two.

Nice one.

...

You go to Sean's friend's house and drop off the other letters and key fob for the lock up. There aren't any police around.

...

You tell Sean to drive back to base camp.

The roads are dark.

And quiet.

You tell him to stop. You get out.

There's a badger. It's been run over. You pick it up by its leg. It's mangled and bloody. You throw it on the windscreen and tell Sean to drive.

You tell them it'll make a nice hat.

Ha

YOU WILL DIE IN FOUR DAYS

Sean goes shopping.

It's Monday morning.

You text him a shopping list with a reminder to get a needle and thread for the badger hat. LOL.

He buys milk, burgers, chicken dippers, water, lamb kebabs, biscuits, cutlery, torches, a couple of phones, a dictaphone, three tapes, a Yorkie bar and a Toffee Crisp.

At base camp Karl cooks. You eat a burger.

Your plan is to steal an X5 [a police vehicle] with all the guns inside. You formulate exit strategies and talk about camera locations and possible public activity, things like that, but what you're thinking, inside your head, is that you'd give anything to have a quiet meal with Sam right now, out here in the countryside, but it's all fucked, properly fucked, and you're going to be on the naughty step for a very long time after all of this. The strange part is, you're actually less stressed today than you were a week ago. It all just feels like a weird video game now, a cross between *Bourne Identity* and *Grand Theft Auto*, like you can do whatever you want, when you want, because people don't see what's really going on. They don't want to see. They just want to live their happy lives. Which is why the police get away with what they get away with, but not anymore. You've read these pleas in the papers, about how they're wanting a reasonable resolution out of this, well there can't possibly be one, because you're a cop killer for a start. Though in fairness, the papers reckon that officer from the other night is fifty-fifty. So there you go. That's life. You're not too fussed about not killing him. You were going to go and finish him off, but it's not really the point. He got two shots. That's enough. At the end of the day, if he's looking a bit of a mess, it might not have been him that's been picking on you, but he can hold the officers that were picking on you responsible. So what do you do now? Every time you think about shooting yourself, which you think about a lot, it's not that you're not able to do it, it's just that somebody else can do it. The weight's been lifted off your head now. It's not a case of having to take a bunch of tablets. You can just go out and keep shooting police officers and eventually you'll get hit. At the end of the day you expect to get sniped. You'll have to get sniped, then it's over. You want it to be over. You don't want to be doing this for ages, because the longer you're doing this the longer you feel the fucking pain, you suppose. So that's what you'll do. You can't turn back what you've done. An idea did come into your head today though. Sean was saying how he's going to write a book about all of this, and him and Karl can sell their story to the highest bidder, because there's plenty of money to be made out of this, and what you thought is, if you get a dictaphone, you can make an audio log and give it to the papers, then people will know the truth, which is why Sean's bought a dictaphone from Argos this morning, so you can sit in the tent, put a tape in and press record [this is an edited and rewritten version of a seventy-six-page typed transcript of recordings you made, containing your thoughts],

This is Raoul Moat on the fifth of July 2009 and this is an audio log. It's a record of what I'm doing, what I'm thinking, and why I'm doing what I'm doing. It's for the public, but it's going to the papers first. I've tried communicating with the police, but they're holding a lot back. As far as I'm concerned the public has a right to know the truth and they will know the truth by the end of this tape. Right, as people are aware, me and Sam started seeing each other in 2005. Well, it was New Year's Eve in 2004, so you could say it was 2004, but either way, we were seeing each other for nearly six years. Before I met Sam I'd always wanted to die, but I wasn't willing to kill myself because my gran put her whole life into bringing me up. If there is an afterlife, which I believe there is, it would piss her off to watch me throw it away, but irrespective of my religious beliefs, I was happy for people to take pot shots at me. I worked my ticket. Kids came in my house with boiler suits and swords and machetes, all kinds of rubbish going on. Back then nobody made me happy, even though I was with some really good women, though this business about Marissa being terrified of me is bollocks. Me and her fought like cat and dog, and okay, I set about her, she got a few clips, which weren't too light either, but she's like a weapon against me [you punched her and throttled her and hit her with a baseball bat, smashed her head with your knee, pushed her into a wall, threatened to hire a hit man to murder her, and left her terrified of you even after your relationship had ended], but anyway, who cares, the thing with Sam was, I liked her way before I went out with her. She was stunning, with lovely hair, great legs, a real head-turner. She used to go down to the Bigg Market, inappropriately dressed, you know. I didn't know how young she was, but she used to come and talk to me on the door. She was seeing someone at the time though, and me being me, I don't want to put my cock where somebody else's is, so I said to get rid of him, which was a double bluff really, but she's stubborn beyond belief, and the second week passed and that was it, time's up, so I started seeing this other woman who was reasonably pretty, but a little on the big side for me. The bottom line is, I'm not a person who settles for second best, so I got this call from Sam on New Year's Eve and we had a good talk. I don't like many women. I don't understand them. But with Sam it was like having a conversation with myself. We decided to go out. We loved each other even before it got physical. It was like out of a textbook, and very quickly she moved in. We were inseparable. It was fantastic. She was jealous, very possessive, which I liked, being honest, but we had a few problems, and it wasn't so much the swearing, but she could be hurtful, quite mean, and there was one day when I lost it and pushed her. It came from nowhere. I didn't expect it. I didn't think I could do it with her, but she hit

88

the floor and split her head. I was fucking gutted to be honest. It showed up straight away in her blonde hair, and obviously she was upset. She was crying. I was upset and pissed off with myself, because I didn't want that with her, so we both calmed down and I said I'd be off if I ever did that to her again, because violence always progresses, a slap turns into a punch, and we'd end up shooting each other. I told her she had to stop getting in my face, and me and her were fine after that. Whenever I had an outburst it was just punching things, anything but her, but the thing is, you can't be smashing up things you've paid £150 for, or hurting your hands, so it became apparent I needed to cut Marissa out of my life. I shouldn't have kept my ex that close. After she was out of the picture the arguments became non-existent and it was fantastic again, though we had a few more break-ups. This thing in the paper pissed me off actually, saying she went to her gran's after getting beaten up. Not at all. The first time she went to her gran's was when I was getting it from both sides, Sam and Marissa, and I got them in the car and said, listen, just get out there and have a fight on that bit of grass, but they're not fighters, they can't fight to save their lives, so it was a stupid thing to do. Two women shouldn't be fighting, but Sam was upset about that and went to her gran's, which is when I sweet-talked her and she came home, but it was nothing to do with domestic violence [Sam said she left because you'd been violent]. Sam was the turning point in my life. I went straight when I met her. I came off the doors. I spent all my time with her. Most days we went out together, and I've got loads of recordings on the computer, going to the coast and the kids being on the horsey beep-beep ride, things like that. Great times. But I got arrested for daft things, like the conspiracy to murder, which sounds terrible, but it was a nonsense, just part of the hunting season on Mr Moat, while others were being protected, and it was around then that I taxed this gun and buried it.

The tape runs out. You turn it over and press record.

Moving on, me and Sam got the house in Fenham, and she gave birth to my daughter. That was a nice experience. I'm a little paranoid where women are concerned. I've seen them at their worst on the doors, but I trusted Sam and enjoyed watching her grow. Even with her huge belly I still fancied the pants off her. She was getting everything ready, a different kind of woman, really upmarket, and I went to the hospital for her to have the baby. It was emotional, nice, a kid born out of love, a good memory. So I came home, and of course there was the inevitable downside. It sounds daft, but Sam mothered me. I need cuddles. I like to lie and have my hair stroked, that kind of thing. It's nice to feel that bond, but inevitably when you have a baby you get pushed out. I got through it though, and suggested opening a business to secure our future together. She had faith in me, because I am a grafter, and if I put my mind to something then anything is possible, so I opened Mr Trimmit, a landscape company. I worked all hours God sends, seven days a week, trying to make it a success, when I could have done any number of things, like gone back into licensed fighting, but Sam didn't want that. She liked the bad boy thing for a while, but she liked this other side of me more. Unfortunately this other side of me is a bit boring. So I opened the company, and before I realised it things were deteriorating. The problem was, like I said, I need my bond. It's not sex. I never had that kind of relationship with Sam. That's not what I was with her for. It was just that she was angry, because she was left on her own while I was away working, so there were fights between me and her, pushing and shoving, that kind of thing, which I'm not proud about. I get funny when I get hurt. The problem of it was, I might be able to control a punch this time, or a slap that time, but she was getting in my face again, and I knew it would progress. I did give her a few clips, but always with an open hand, never with a fist, and she hurts me more with her mouth than I hurt her with my fist [she said in court that you stamped on her and dragged her by her hair and throttled her]. I took time off work to be with her, but I didn't want to let the business go. I should have closed it and romanced her again properly, but on January the thirteenth of last year I came back to the house from work and she'd gone. The only two people I ever cared about are my gran and Sam, on equal levels. I don't give a shit about anybody else. My kids, yeah, but I've no interest in other adults. I was devastated. I tried my magic, but got nowhere. On Valentine's Day I got close, but she pulled away. My heart sank. I tried to address it. I didn't push her though, because sex has to be given, so I took her home and it was in limbo. Now I'm funny about truth and honesty. I don't like fucking liars. But Sam asked a few times if I'd cheated on her while we were split up. I told her I'd met a couple of girls and always said no, but Sam never quite believed it, probably because she knew what I was like before her, when

I always had three or four women on the go. The way I tried to explain it to her was that I'd changed. I told her the way I used to see women was, I'd put a hundred fishing rods out to catch ninety-nine small fish and one whopper, because back then I thought if I only put one fishing rod out at a time I might waste much of my life waiting for that whopper. But now I'd caught that whopper, which was Sam, and there was no way I was going to let it go. So it occurred to me that there are these things in the Yellow Pages where you can ring up and do a lie detector test. I thought it would make a nice little present for Sam, which I wish I'd never mentioned, but anyway, time progressed and I started to deteriorate, because she'd say things like she wanted me out of her life, which meant I was crying a lot, and it's terrible to say, really terrible, because I love my kids, but Sam comes before anything, and it's more than love. It's something else. It's probably something depraved. Then it was June, and that's when the allegation of assault [on a child] came. Obviously it's not worth going into. I've given my account. Whether people believe me is entirely up to them. As far as I'm concerned the medical evidence proves I didn't do it. I've been punching people for years and whenever I punch them they get a huge amount of swelling, so there's no possible way I could have hit a child and not caved them in. It's just common sense. But the witch-hunts started and the police stuck their oar in and all the rest of it, and I've ended up being hanged for something I didn't do, and I'm pissed off, because I've had enough trouble off the police, arresting me for things I didn't do, and now I'm seeing these things in the paper, like the sword in my car boot, which this is the thing, right, that sword was just an unsharpened sword going to a collector's because it had a snake on it which scared the girls so I was getting it out the house. Then there's this knuckleduster thing, which is I allegedly had a knuckleduster, but there's no way, because I'd kill someone with a knuckleduster if I hit them with it, look at the size of me, so during the interview I told the officer I wanted a swipe done on my hands for metal fragments to prove I'd never had any metal on them, rings or anything, but to cut a long story short, they were saying I'd jumped on this guy's head, even though I didn't even want to fight in the first place as I was a bit knackered actually, and anyway, these things always fell apart when it got to court, like the knuckleduster didn't even fit on my hand, but I've been pulled over one hundred and eighty-four times [again, Northumbria Police recorded you being pulled over fourteen times between 2000 and 2010], and it shows there are officers targeting me for whatever reasons.

The tape runs out. You put a second tape in and press record.

This is Raoul Moat again. July 2010. So, coming to the cars now, which is basically some daft lad who took the number plate off my car for whatever reason, so I put it in the windscreen until I could get more sticky things, and the next thing I know is, I'm rewinding my tapes. The CCTV by the way is for protection against the police, because they'd arrest me for some pretty amazing things if I didn't have it. I'm well aware they might plant something in my garden. People don't want to know the police are like that, but that's my opinion. They've tried everything but leaving cheese out to get me off the streets.

The bottom line is I wake up and there's a ticket on my car, so I rewind my tapes and they're going over my car, which is why I go straight to Etal Lane police station and put in a complaint, asking why they've got nothing better to do, with crackheads and smackheads and all kinds of shit going on at that estate, and next thing is, my car's been uplifted. So I'm fired up, and I'm shouting and bawling on the phone, and I go up to the station saying the car's been crushed, well, not crushed, but I'm telling them how it's in a million bits now, totally smashed, and they tell me I've got to go up to Ponteland, so I go up there and get some smarmy cunt, blah, blah, blah, saying it didn't have a tax on the window. Fair enough, it had been vandalised at the time and had a smashed windscreen, and what it was is, I'd taken the lights out the back in case they got smashed, because I had a rick with somebody at the time who was a bit of a crazy gunman, so there'd also been a crowbar put over the windscreen and the top of the roof [all this damage had happened before the police took your vehicle away], big fucking deal, and the copper's attitude was just like, fuck off. Moving on to the more serious stuff in my criminal history. The conspiracy to murder beggars belief. That was in about 1999 [it was in 2000]. I remember being in the house when they pulled me in and it was like the *Terminator*, just about every cop outside the house, and they said to exit one at a time. I came out last, and apparently I'd conspired to murder this guy, but obviously I'm not worried because I haven't conspired to murder anybody. So that's that, which is boring. I was locked up for five days I think, and they love to do things like not give you any water so you've got to drink out the toilet. Well fuck that, I don't give a monkey's, I'll drink out the toilet. They put you in the hottest cell so you sweat your knackers off, but I'm not bothered. It's nothing compared to Spain. Anyway, I got interviewed and it's not worth discussing really. They had nothing on me. Their story was I was planning on going to this location to shoot this guy, and apparently I set a shotgun off down the phone. My argument was it could have been a balloon bursting, but supposedly I threatened to shoot him and they were arguing that I was going to lead him to this spot. So they raided my house and pulled it to bits, footmarks up the wall, on the sofa, bin bags emptied — trashed, basically. The next thing is, they try to send me to court without footwear. Now by law I have to have footwear in court. I think that's how the law works anyway, so I said that to them, and in the end they gave me shoes, size six, even though I'm size twelve, and me being me, I just chewed the backs off and used them as flip-flops. In court they were talking about putting me on remand before a trial, but the story sounded ridiculous because you don't go from normal citizen to blasting anyone [this is your version of what happened] so I got an NFA [the CPS withdrew the charges]. Next thing is I'm working as a doorman and this woman keeps making a beeline for me, offering me drinks at night and things. Well, I've been teetotal since I was seventeen because I need my inhibitions, without them there are problems. So she's asking me about the doors and fights and violence, and something's not right, which is why I start digging. Next thing is, my friend tells me he thinks she's involved with the police, so I spin her a line and tell her that some guy got my girlfriend pregnant and how I'm going to take him fishing off the rocks at Whitley Bay and he'll have himself a little tumble, no forensics. Next I rang another mate and got him to ring me, to create a theory of conspiracy, but I didn't tell my girlfriend or the guy I was saying had got her pregnant, because they might not have gone along with it. Anyway, it worked like a charm. The police were all over it. Whether my friend said anything to anybody, I don't know, but I'm convinced it was this woman [you don't know what happened]. She tried to defend herself and I just smirked and she let rip, saying I was born with nothing and the police would make sure I had nothing for the rest of my life. Well she didn't say police, but I knew where the message was coming from, and I found out the hard way, because they've been mucking my life up ever since. I lost my job on the doors because of the police, after I kept gripping them [that's what you believed, but there's no evidence for it]. They're the biggest army there is, the biggest gang in town, that's what they say, worse than doormen. Half of them were bullied at school, just prom leftovers, shagging each other's wives, drowning them in the bath and all that shit, and there were other things the police arrested me for, I'm just trying to think of them. Oh yeah, this traffic warden I supposedly assaulted. I used to pull up outside Sam's work. She worked at a hairdresser, so to save parking halfway across town I'd pull up and just wait, where this traffic warden was. Anyway, about a year later I was driving along the bottom of the Bigg Market and I said to my friend, look, there's that tosser, and my mate's daft so he shouts something about how this traffic warden should get a proper job, you fucking mug. So this warden comes over and he's putting his head in the window and I'm winding the window up on him, and unfortunately I put my hand on his back, so I try to drive round him to leave, and the next thing I know is, I've got the cuffs on and I'm in the back of the van, so obviously Sam is crying her eyes out, she's hysterical, which is why I'm getting rowdy in the van. Down at the station I get interviewed, and it goes to court, and there are these inch-high private eyes, and obviously nobody's going to believe I was doing anything other than trying to defuse the situation, so I got let off [this is your version of what happened]. But this is just skimming the surface. The main thing is, there's a law for the public and a law for Raoul, and the law for Raoul is I cannot defend myself. A herd of wildebeest with flick-knives can try to do me in and I just have to stand there and take it. Anyway, that's all rubbish. My main problem with the police is I've gone straight with Sam yet they've hounded me. They even came to my door, after the charge, saying they've got information that leads them to believe I'm in danger [you were asked to visit the police station, where you were warned that a person or persons may want to cause you physical harm, though the police wouldn't give you any more details other than saying it was nothing to do with the current charge against you; it's called an Osman warning]. Well, unless it's Martians invading, I can't see what that was about, so I was asking if I'm going to be shot or stabbed or what, or if it's just fisticuffs, trying to get more disclosures really, but they wouldn't say anything, which isn't much help. It's not like I haven't made enemies, like this guy who I went to the station about this other time, because unfortunately his car had burst into flames, I'm not sure how that happened, but the police came round saying they saw me drive away, which is impossible, because like I told them, the camera at my house proved it couldn't be me. Anyway, they gave me this warning that I was in danger, but all they've done is get me winding myself up in the house [a few days later you called the police officer who delivered the warning and told her you thought they were deliberately provoking you into starting a fight with someone, at which point they would then arrest you, proving that you were out of control and violent, and you told her the timing would be perfect for Northumbria Police, describing it as the cherry on top of the case; she said the warning had nothing to do with the current case and assured you there was no hunting season on Mr Moat]. And at the same time, funnily enough, a lot of my friends were becoming informants. I nearly caught one of them because he was getting these funny cheques at his house. When I asked about it he said it was benefits, but it looked like the wrong colour. Also, this woman who's sweet to me came over one day and said my house was going to get raided. I'd noticed the helicopter following me actually. So I ditched my friends around then. It was just me and Sam after that, the way I like it.

The tape stops. You turn it over.

The psychologists said I can't be helped, even though I'm really intelligent. They wrote me off. But to me, it's not about a psychologist saying, look, you're not a lunatic, you're just twisted and fucked, we can't do anything with you. Instead they should sit there and work with me, but none of them have done that. They've just done a witch-hunt. At the end of the day, if I'm wrong in ways I don't understand I want that sorted. I can't have it sorted now. It's too late. They never gave me a chance. As far as I'm concerned they're lying, all conspiring, I do believe that. I don't believe for one minute I'm as wrong as they're saying. Well, I am now, but this is part of why I've gone a bit fucking daft. This is what they wanted me to be, but I treasured Sam more than anything, and that's the direction I would have gone I think. I couldn't have lived without Sam. I always knew that. So I went to court and told them to shove their deal up their arse. I told my barrister it was over, no point in fighting anymore, because they're all just bullies. I'd take the jail instead. It's no holiday camp though. The cells stink. They're smaller than a dog's kennel, and the beds are piffling things. When you're a big guy it feels like you're going to snap your head off, and meal times are pathetic. I couldn't hack it really, not then. If I went to jail now I could hack it, because I've nothing anymore. That's why I came out and got my vengeance. Now I can just take the shootout and everybody's happy, everybody's got their vengeance, and I'm quite content. But back then I was thinking about Sam constantly, all day. The police will spin it and say it's obsession. Maybe love is obsession. People talk about stalking. When me and Sam split up I used to go round and give her flowers and talk to her every day, but that's not stalking to me, it's showing I love her and care. Stalking is when you follow someone around and are just being a nob. That's unhealthy. If people want to call what I had with Sam an obsession, call it an obsession, but it's not what I'd call it. I'd call it a deep-seated love, a little bit down to lacking parts of my personality, missing her, needing her, that kind of thing. I couldn't take her out of my mind. It's a happy place. She's a drug to me. If this situation is ever going to resolve itself, it's going to be through Sam, but I don't think that'll happen. It's inevitable what'll happen at this stage. But anyway, I was in jail and I got myself a job sweeping floors, because I'm a hard worker. The same mundane thing each day though, and I can't hack that kind of routine, because I'm an intelligent guy, I get bored, and that brings on aggression, and with that comes problems. So I was in jail and I heard these rumours [which are false], and she visited me and I went to give her a kiss, but she wouldn't let me. I think she gave up when I got found guilty to be honest. I'm not a forceful guy, because with a girlfriend that'll never be forgotten, but sometimes I am a little more forceful and I get annoyed, but when I was inside I heard about this Chris Brown, which really does piss me off, and it's taken a lot away from what I think about Sam. I put her on a pedestal and don't want to think of her like that. I blame him. I know it's her as well, but I blame him. It's probably why I've done a lot of the things I've done. If it's happened. I might be barking up the wrong tree [she wasn't seeing Chris until after she broke up with you]. So I'm inside, and I've been let down by Sam, and she comes for the visit saying it's over and all the rest of it, really tearful, which upset me, seeing her cry, and I'm also not getting my retrial, so I'm fucking pissed off with the police, wondering whether to blow up Etal Lane police station, and very early on it's becoming clear that I've got a problem with being banged up. I hate the idea of being locked in a room, probably from being constantly grounded as a kid. It brought back all these memories I tend not to think about, and it just

100

dragged me down. You've got two types of people in jail. You've got scum, just little charvers who deserve to have nothing, because no matter what you do, they'll just be shitbags. Then you've got your normal, regular lads, who've fucked up, made one mistake, often drugs, and everybody thinks just bang them up, but jail should be a last resort. It costs £120 a day from what I understand, and that's just taxpayers' money wasted. It's not productive. They'd be better off sending me to Afghanistan, then I'd have some pride, I'd be doing something worthwhile. A lot of people agree with me on that. There's no rehabilitation for me. All I've done is come out and do this. Anyway, me and Sam argued when she visited, and next thing is she wouldn't answer the phone, then she came on the phone saying it's over, and how apparently I've slept with a stripper. I'm not a crybaby, but this situation had me fucked. I said, okay, find this stripper, because I've not been seeing a stripper, and I offered that lie detector test. I said I'd come out and fix everything, and the thing with it is, she didn't even know this, but I was thinking about coming out and getting back into the unlicensed fighting, £1000 a fight. There were lots of things like that, nice little surprises for her, because I just wanted her to have everything, you know. But it had me fucked. It's just everything over the last year really. I probably underestimated how knackered I was when I went to jail. They took the most important bit of my life, the queen on the chessboard, so it was inevitable that this would happen. These bastards stitched me up. They caused this. I might be funny in the head, and maybe I'm potentially capable of doing this anyway, but when they take all the cards off the table, of course this would happen. Being honest, there are times I wanted Sam to move on and be happy, but I cannot do it, I cannot do it, not in a million years. I'm fucking screwed. It's ridiculous. I feel like King Kong when he's at the top of that flaming building, you know. I'm all messed up. But that's the situation, I'm in jail and I've got to write Sam off, especially when she says she's got a boyfriend, and from what I understand he's a cop [he wasn't, but Sam said he was], and he's been posted up here from down south. He must have been besotted with her. Probably it's a relationship through the internet, something on Facebook [she met him while he was handing out flyers for karate lessons]. So that's the situation. I'm inside, and I heard something about motorbikes, and something to do with taekwondo, so I've got these pieces of a jigsaw, trying to put it together, driving myself nuts. Sam's not a slapper, so she must have been hurting. I get out of jail and it's a fucking mess. My house isn't the house I remember. It's like a carbon copy of my house, but not a good one. The grass is long. The hedge needed cutting. There's rubbish everywhere. The floors needed a good scrub. Sam used to have it immaculate when she was there. Then I'm trying to talk to her on the phone and she gets mean, saying I can't go to her house, and how he's a police officer and he'll put me on my arse, and it made me feel shit, because I'm well aware that I'm past my prime, which I've always felt was a fucking mean trick, finding Sam at the end of my youth. So she's going, nah, nah, nah, winding me up, and I don't feel well by the way. Shooting that copper the other day felt like some kind of *Doom* game. It's obviously affected me. I've got two hostages here, and they say I don't half grind my teeth in my sleep. The hostages are fine by the way. They're not in danger,

102

but they don't really know that. Anyway, Sam's giving me hell on the phone, got me in tears at one point, saying don't go down there, how he's an officer of the law. So this guy is in the way the whole time, and an idea's forming. If he'd been anyone else this wouldn't have happened, but Sam's on the phone again, asking why I'm across at her house, and my phone runs out, so I flew home, grabbed a charger and the gun, and Karl was with me. I made him come. He didn't want to be part of it. But I phoned her back and she's saying I never went to jail for her, and she denied the conversation about getting a retrial ever happened, even swore on my daughter's life that it never happened, which hurt, because I don't swear on a child's life to that, and she's saying we've been finished for months, but the bottom line is, she's saying hurtful things, which is why I said I'd fight him right now, thinking that if I win I'm a cunt, but at least I've got my dominance, and if I lose, then Sam'll relax a bit. It's a win-win situation. So I've gone across. And I'm sorry about shooting her. I read that she was critical, but she'll live now, so I'm pleased about that. She's set for life. I miss her though. I never wanted this. But I am what I am, and there's only one thing left to do. I'm not on the run. Friends advised me to leave. I've got zero contact with them now by the way. But I'm not leaving. I'm not going to France or Ireland. I'm staying to fight the only fight that's left to fight, and that's with the police, who are rubbish by the way, because I've been right under their fucking noses a long time and they haven't got a clue. I move around. I'm never far away. And from what I understand the social worker and a few other arseholes are in hiding. Well they caused this. You can kill someone a long time before you ever punch them or hurt them or stab them. You can kill somebody without ever going near them. That's what they did to me. They took everything from me. The minute they took Sam away they killed me. But what the police are putting in the newspapers is a pack of lies. I never jumped on Sam's belly [she says you did]. There's been pushing and shoving, a few open hands, but very rare [she says you dragged her by the hair and throttled her]. Get all these other fuckers on the lie detectors as well. That's the reason I had cameras, for my own protection against all these liars, big liars, lie, lie, lie, so this is my thing, this is where I break my own rules and I've got a bit of a problem with myself to be honest. From now on, for each lie I see in the paper, any paper, I'm going to kill an innocent member of the public, right. I'll phone up and let them know which lie pissed me off and I want each person who's told this lie to go on a lie detector, right. Those are my rules. And if they don't do this, right, if people don't comply, I'll just continue killing people, it's as simple as that.

The tape ends. You put the third tape in.

This is Raoul Moat on the fifth of July 2010, continued, tape number three. As I was saying, I've got a bit of a problem with what happened to Sam. I didn't mean to hurt her. My intention was just to make her very wealthy for the rest of her life. But he's turned her into something I didn't want her to be. She's better than that. This kid was an arse, but he's dead now, so he looks a bit stupid. Here's something — I'm hearing he had an iron bar. I didn't notice it on the night, but he's brought that to a fight, a fair fight, where I'm supposed to be evenly matched, in fact he's supposed to be bigger than me, yet he's brought an iron bar. Well I brought a gun, ha ha ha. Anyway, he clearly wasn't after a fair fight. He's not a fair person. That paints his character. Whatever kind of instructor he's supposed to be, he obviously felt he was going to get his arse kicked. So he's no hero. And I'm pissed off with this story about me shooting Sam first. I didn't shoot her first, and he didn't chase me. He ran away like a fucking gutless carrot [after you shot him], and I gave chase and shot him. I've no qualms about it. He deserved it. It's amazing how the mighty fall when Mr Moat turns up. Speaking of which, yes, I did smash Terry's windows. So fucking what? What's good for one is good for the other. But the papers have made me out to be a cunt. I'm a killer, fair enough, I'll take my hat off to that, but there's no way I domestically abused Sam, not in the way they're talking about it [Sam and her family say you did]. So there you go. Every time they print a fucking lie, watch what happens. I've spent the last couple of days pondering what to do. I was worried Sam would die, because if she dies it's for nothing, but the bottom line is, the bit I don't understand — she shouldn't have taunted me. I've had to really think about that. She couldn't have known it would come to this. She would never have believed I'd shoot her. I read in the papers that he's not a police officer, well fuck that, I know he is. She knew it would provoke a reaction, and when it gets to that stage it doesn't matter whether someone's a rocket ship or whatever. I proved that's the case the other night with the officer in his T5. By the way, it doesn't matter which officers go into hiding, because my theory is they work as a unit, a collective bunch of shitbags. I've only met one or two decent officers in my time. One was from Etal Lane. He treats everyone with respect and I'll give him credit for that, but the majority are turds, especially the women. So it doesn't matter whether I killed the right one, it's all the same person as far as I'm concerned. One thing I've noticed is there are no bobbies on the beat. I'm expecting the crime rate to go up, but that's not my intention. It's amazing how they scurry and hide when someone fights back. That's the thing about liars, they like to hide. I don't hide. My conclusion is that after all the times they've taken the piss, all the cars they've taken, the relationships they've wrecked, the times they've stitched me up, everything they've done, they're finally taking me seriously. And this thing in the paper about shooting my kneecaps, they'd be foolish to try that because I'll carry on shooting as long as I'm alive. I wish I could have been a better bloke for Sam. I'm an intelligent kid. I could have done so many amazing things with my life. I could have made her life so much better. But people like the police demoralise me. That's what bullies do. Also, this thing about people saying I'm crazy with cameras all over the place. Probably I am a bit paranoid, but it's because I always expected something from them. I never saw how they could take my family from me, but I remember PC 190 making that comment in the back of his T5 [he pulled you over and confiscated your vehicle because you didn't have insurance to carry scrap metal]. I was telling him he'd taken everything off me and they could just fuck off [it was David Rathband, who you later shot, though you never realised it was the same officer]. He said I still had my business

106

and my family, and I remember thinking at the time, how could they take more off me than they already had? Well I've found out good and proper. My theory's always been that I can't stop the police planting drugs in my house, or a firearm in my car. They could just get a bag out my bin with prints on it, or a tub, and put crack in it, Bob's your uncle. That's what I've been anticipating. They never got round to it, but they tried everything else. I can't believe they had me in jail for this thing with the assault. I'd been straight, working hard, paying my taxes, doing the right thing, not cheating on my woman, and I get fucked more than any other time in my life. It's a clear sign that the criminal way is the best for me, but it's not something I want to go back to. I can't now. One other thing, just to be clear, I've got no interest in Sam's family. I was very tempted to shoot her mother, but that's Sam's mum, and Sam needs her. I want Sam to have a happy life. I don't expect any kind of thank you from her for that. The crazy part is I've given her more opportunities than I ever could have given her if I'd been straight. This country's crazy for that. The harder you work, the more you get fucked. The more you're a nob, the more you get. Me and Sam worked hard. Just because she stayed at home doesn't mean she didn't work hard. She worked really hard. She did all the housework and looked after the kids. That's a job in itself, and she deserves more from life than I could give her, but what I've done gives her the chance of a decent life. She'll meet somebody else. To be honest, he wasn't what I'd expected. He didn't look big and chiselled. He looked podgy. And he wasn't particularly good-looking. She can do a lot better than that. She can do better than me. Soon she'll be minted and do very well for herself. I've looked out for her. One thing I am worried about is my kids — whether they're going to get picked on and bullied. There are downsides to this I never thought about. I'm apprehensive about their future. One thing I know is that doing my duty was never going to be good for me. Unfortunately I was in a position where I loved my woman more than anything else. I could have done all the right things, but the heart would still have been empty. I feel guilty about that. It sounds selfish, but that's not quite how it is. Anyway, I can't profit from my crimes, but I don't see why the people I love should suffer. So taking care of my loved ones, including Sam, that's the priority at the minute. The idea came from reading all this rubbish in the paper from people saying I pointed the gun at them. They're after compensation. Everybody was a hero that night apparently, but if anybody had got involved or tried to tackle me they would have been shot. It's as simple as that. The coast was clear. I had a damn good check. Everybody cowered in their houses. Rightly so. I can't criticise them for that. They'll all be quids in now though. It's like the lottery coming. The only one who doesn't profit is me. Well, at least I get a certain satisfaction that everybody's taken care of. Every cloud has a silver lining. Every reaction has an equal and opposite reaction. Something good comes from every bad. I've been thinking about that a lot. Now it's just a case of me doing my thing. It's not that I'm frightened of going to jail. It's just common sense. It's no good for me. That three months in there hasn't helped. If they put me in there for fifty years a lot of people will be getting done in. At £120 a day of taxpayers' money, that's no good for anything. It's been a strange day. I've been to the shop. People are walking past and not batting a fucking eyelid. I didn't think I'm the kind of person who blends in. I'm plastered all over the front pages, but not one person's recognised me. It's been a nice change being out here. It's quite peaceful.

A car horn beeps. Birds chirp. You press stop.

...

It's 10pm. The three of you get in the car. Sean drives.

...

You want food, but you've got no money. You tell Sean to look for somewhere quiet to rob. You see a chippy in Seaton Delaval.

It looks empty.

Sean drives past a couple of times.

He parks in the alley behind it. You get out.

You've got the gun.

You walk to the front door of the shop and go inside. There are no customers, just an Asian guy with a moustache.

You point the gun at him and shout,

Give me the money!

He looks terrified. He gives you £100.

Easy.

You walk out the front door and go round the corner to the alley, but the shop guy is in the alley too. He must have come out the back door. You point the gun at him and shout,

Come on, then!

He goes back inside. You get in the car and laugh. Sean puts his foot down and you throw a handful of notes at Karl,

Wonga.

You fancy a KFC.

…

Sean drives to Blyth, but the guy on the speaker says they're closed and you shout,

Fuck off!

Sean drives away.

…

Let's go get a Maccy D's.

Sean drives to McDonald's in Ashington. It's open. He orders at the hatch, two large Chicken Select meals with chilli dips, a Diet Coke for you, Coke for Karl, Big Tasty meal with Coke for Sean and three Yorkie McFlurry ice creams. He parks facing the exit.

…

You eat. Another car pulls up, just some girls.

…

There's a police station around the corner.

…

You see a police car drive past. You say,

Will I get him?

But you don't. You're busy eating your McFlurry.

…

Sean starts driving back to Rothbury. A police car follows you, but pulls off after half a mile.

Lucky bastard.

You do nothing.

Your mood has changed.

YOU WILL DIE IN THREE DAYS

Tuesday. 9am.

Sean's at the car, or near the car, or he was supposed to be, but he's calling you. He says the police are at the car. You tell him to hurry back, get to the tent, throw everything in the bushes.

Karl helps him.

...

You walk towards the car, hiding in the trees. There are armed police around it.

...

You call Sean and Karl and tell them to head downriver.

You go into the trees.

...

You call them again. They're fine.

...

You call again. They don't answer.

It's 10.06am.

You head east.

You stay under the trees.

You keep going.

The helicopter's in the sky.

You hide in the woods.

...

You wait.

...

You've got a tumble-dryer stomach, lying here, checking off all the things you left at base camp — the dictaphone and the tapes, they're the main things, hopefully they'll get to the press.

116

What else?

The letter to Sam. Fucking hell.

…

You stay hidden.

…

At least she'll be able to sell her story. There'll be books written about all this, and you'll be made out to be some crazed fucking maniac, but she'll be set for life.

…

She'll make a fortune off this.

…

But you can't stop thinking about her, because the thing you don't understand is, she knew that other side of you, the side you keep buried. Only she can control it, make it go away, bring it back, because it's like the Hulk, but more than anger, and it only comes out when you get hurt, and she really hurt you this time, being mean, really quite mean, abusing you. You heard it when you were outside that window with the gun, listening to them slagging you off, and you can always tell when she's got an audience because she's even more of

Leabharlanna Fhine Gall

a cunt, very hurtful, cutting you in two, but you wish you hadn't shot her.

...

You looked around for anyone else to shoot, but there was nobody, just Sam.

...

At least you don't need to die worrying about her.

...

She'll have a good life now.

...

You were setting her up for life.

...

Making sure she got compensation.

...

There's no going back with her now.

...

Going back isn't an option.

You're committed.

It's just a case of doing your thing.

They did this to you.

…

They bullied you.

…

Wherever you went, wherever you worked, they were spoiling it, every good woman chased away under advisement by some police officer doing a PNC check in front of her with their radio turned up full, your kids in tears, you and Sam hounded, negative comments, and it would have been fair enough years ago, but not now, uplifting your vehicles, arrests for violence you didn't do, yet the stuff you did do you didn't get arrested for. It's been a sorry state of affairs. And like with all bullying, it affects your frame of mind. It affected how you behaved with Sam. Not violence, but losing your spark for fun living. You miss her, you really fucking miss her and you're never going to see her again. It fucking hurts. You wish you could turn the clock back. Because you never wanted this. You and her used to be like Siamese twins. You could have lived a normal life with Sam, you really do believe that. She would have loved it round here, though not the spiders and stuff because Sam's all hair and nails and spider, eek. Like, if you ever wanted to get some peace you'd go in the shed because spiders were guaranteed in there. She'd have liked living in the sticks though. You and her talked about getting a place out here, either buying a place or going privately rented, which is what you would have done probably, on the lease. You saw this one house which had a bit of farmland, and it would have been ideal. Because you're a bit of a farmer type. People probably realise that. It comes from the French side of your family. They've been into farming for years. The truth is, you never got used to the city, not at all, even after twenty years, with all the hustle and bustle and traffic jams, but when the family moved to England they went straight to Fenham, so you've spent the best part of your life there. Well you moved around a bit, up and down the country [you've lived in Fenham all your life, but you told people otherwise, including a psychiatrist and social workers]. You ended up back in Fenham because of the good schools for the kids, but you knew you needed your space, so you and Sam were looking for a place out here, because she could have had her horses, and you'd have land for your animals, dogs and rabbits and stuff, which you've always liked the idea of, having your animals. Maybe that's something you got from your gran. She got you into all that. She had a pond with koi carp in it, a couple of ducks too, though the ducks didn't last long. The council probably told her to get rid of them. But you used to feed the fish and put frogspawn in the pond, and you and Tony [Tony Laidler, who lived down the street and is still a good friend] would catch tadpoles in the Pond of Life and put them in Gran's pond, and the two of you would go on adventures all over Newcastle, hunting for little beasties. You'd catch wasps [and put them in jars, and make them fight or drown them]. You'd catch spiders and put them in the road to see whose got squashed first. It was just kids' stuff. Or you'd get all the eggs from different nests and put them in one nest, or take them home and tell your gran the nest had been abandoned, and she'd try to incubate them, and sometimes you went up to the golf course to find baby shrews around the edge of the golf course to take home [but one night you put them in your bed and forgot about them and when you fell asleep you squashed them]. You used to go all over the place exploring and fishing. You were an outdoors kid, really. You used to come up here, to the river at Rothbury, catching minnows, literally a stone's throw from here, staying at a caravan. That's a great holiday for a kid to go on, because you make loads of friends on a holiday like that, and sometimes you'd skip school to come up here. The thing of it is, your schoolwork probably did suffer, though anyone will say you're a clever kid. You had a cat for a bit. It was called Kitty, a ginger female, which is unusual, because usually they get torn to pieces by the male for being a freak, but that cat died when you moved into your mum's house [when you were about ten], and you got another cat after that, but it died as well. And you had a bullfrog. You can remember because when you and Angus argued over whether it was South American or North American, Uncle Charlie asked whether it was wearing a Stetson or a sombrero. Ha. And you wanted hamsters, but Mum and Brian said no [so you got some anyway and hid them in the garage, but when Brian found them he came upstairs and you ended up crying and you couldn't keep them].

...

You get up off the ground. You've got a gun. You stay under the trees. You walk to the crags. You hide.

...

You and Angus used to come up here. You'd come at the weekend with other kids, getting the bus. You'd bring a rifle and catapult to shoot rabbits. Really, you shot fence-posts and trees more than anything else. You'd borrow equipment from the scout hut [you were both in the scouts] and you had to make sure you got back to Rothbury high street by about 5pm, because that was when the last bus left, and if you missed it there was basically no way back. You missed it once. You and Angus and this other kid were up here, after doing some hiking or something, and you went to this local pub. You had your hair in braids, like the British Bulldog, and Angus was a grunge kid so had his hair long and black, and you went in this pub, which was full of locals. It was like one of those old westerns where everything went quiet. They all left and went off to another room, and you thought, well, fuck that, so you went to a different pub where the people were a lot nicer, and there was a guy at the bar who looked exactly like Andy Bell from Erasure. You being you, you started singing the victim of love one they did, and Angus and this other kid had to bundle

122

you out, but you'd missed the bus by then, so you all sat on this bench next to the war memorial, and this local copper came over asking what you were up to. You'd been drinking and were underage so you stayed quiet until you threw up by his feet and said to him,

Stormy at sea ...

Angus thought it was hilarious. You and Angus were close as kids, but he changed. He's certainly the most intelligent bloke you've ever met [he's three years older than you and you've got the same mum but different dads]. The funny thing is, he had everything going for him. He was like a rhino, a little bulldog, and he used to be into boxing and the weights, and you were jealous of him when you were young. He's a respectable kid, but he went to university and it was the worst thing he ever did, because he became an arse after that, an absolute arse. He had it all, and when you've got that kind of intelligence you can have the best of everything — the top class jobs and all that — but he spent all his time being angry at the wrongs of the world and he blew it [he's doing fine, living in Newcastle, with a good job and friends].

...

[Someone breaks into houses near Rothbury, but the police aren't certain that it was you.]

...

You're not going to get much sleep. You don't need sleep. It's quiet. You cover yourself with bits of trees and leaves. You lie in a dip in the ground. You keep thinking. Think. Think. Think. There are snakes out here. You saw them when you were cutting down trees at Kielder. They'd lie on the stumps in the sunshine.

...

These trees were massive. You took some of the logs home to use as fuel in an open fire, because the plan was to have zero bills in winter, then use the rest to build an adventure playground for the kids [you never built an open fire or an adventure playground].

...

You promised the kids a farm out here. You promised they'd be able to have rabbits, like they had in Fenham, before all the rabbits caught myxomatosis and their eyes turned pink and swelled up, and they were falling over, like they were drunk, a horrible way to go. It would have been like *Of Mice and Men*. Sam would have had her horses, you'd have bred dogs, and you just needed a few more contracts so you could get a bit more money in, like you had when you were on the doors, because that's your job as a dad, and nobody can say you're not a grafter, you know how to work. You started Mr Trimmit from nothing, just got up one morning with the lawnmower and started knocking on doors. And the truth is, if you do

124

the hours you get the money, but it's not an easy lifestyle. Not like on the doors. But you can't do the doors if you've got kids, because things come back to your house. You never know when trouble's coming. Which is why you put everything into Mr Trimmit, because it's what you always wanted to do, ever since you were a kid, when you were wanting to go to agricultural college after school, but it didn't work out so you went to Vickers to make tanks, then a welding company, yet people never say Raoul Moat the engineer or Raoul Moat the tree surgeon, it's always Raoul Moat the doorman. But anyway, you're a grafter, and you were working all hours trying to make Mr Trimmit work, because you didn't want to be skint forever, but the thing is, the recession smashed it to bits, and if there's anything people can put off spending money on when they're pinching their purse it's a tree, you know, because a tree's not going anywhere, so that's why work dropped off, and being fair, you were still putting the hours in, but it moved over to the recovery work, because you're a grafter, and you'll make a job, but again, more problems, which is what you've realised over the past few years, that if you're polite over here you get taken advantage of, badly, which is what happened when you were buying this trailer on eBay. You used to go on there all the time to keep your fingers in any amount of pies. People laugh, but one time you bought ten thousand sets of locking nuts for two and a half grand. It was bankrupt stock and some of it had been flooded, so the packaging was damaged. People said you were mad, and you can remember your girlfriend's mum at that time going bonkers, but in three months you made ten grand off that. eBay was like a little marketplace, and one time you won a recovery trailer, an ex-AA one, heavy-duty, with the tilt bed and everything, and you went down to pick it up. Now if a kid's fair then you're fair. You'll have your little bit of investigation, but you're not going to sit and pull it apart. So this guy was like a Norman Wisdom gypsy type, and you paid seven hundred and fifty quid. That's not a bad price. It was worth a thousand pounds all day long. But what you noticed was, instead of discussing things he was giving you his sales patter. The way you thought about it was, you don't exactly look friendly, so if they're daft enough to sell to a big man like you then they're bringing it on their own head. But you were driving it home, and every time you hit the brakes it's going into the back of the hitch. So you got home and start pulling it apart, and it turned out the brake cables were slack and it was all fused together. That needed to be replaced. Then you noticed the tyres weren't even commercial. And when you looked in the brake drum there were no contents. Fucking hell. That's not right. So you phoned him up. No answer. You sent a message through eBay. Nothing. The thing is, people are learning. What he'd done was insist that you pay him through his daughter's account, which you didn't like. So you sent him an email, and the daughter's giving it how he's away. What that means is you have to wait another week, by which time you'll not be protected, right. So you put in a claim with PayPal and they've just quashed it. Next thing is you phone up and get some Pakistani on the phone and they can't understand a word you're saying, which is why you told them to put someone on who can speak English, and this team manager comes on, and you explain the situation, and what they said was you're not covered because you haven't

126

paid the full amount through PayPal [that's your recollection]. Another one you got hit with was this spoiler you bought to go on a Subaru Impreza. You saw it on there and ordered it, but when it turned up you couldn't believe it, because it was off a fucking Tonka toy. Like, is this for real? You were fuming, so you phoned the guy, as you do, kicking off. You paid a hundred and twenty five quid for this thing, but he just said, look in the description mate. You get stitched up in this country, and there's nothing Trading Standards can do. It's like the trailer thing. You could have been an arse about it and pulled the trailer to pieces in front of him, and re-haggled, but you don't, because it's politeness. It's not in your culture to be like that, but this is how it works in this country now. You never used to have any bother, but it's different these days. The thing is, nobody likes to be lied to, nobody likes to get taken advantage of, and it's a disgrace to be honest, because you worked solid for two years, up at 5am and 6am every morning, grafting sixteen hours a day to get down to London and back some days, wanting it, wanting it, wanting it, but it crippled the family, and like you said to the council, it's not that you want to be treated like an idiot, but you take the stress of the world on your shoulders, the stress of your family, and all you wanted was to be able to ask for help, but you blinked and missed it, and suddenly the kids had grown up and you didn't have enough time with Sam, the kids, all of it, and everything just broke down.

YOU WILL DIE IN TWO DAYS

...

It's quiet.

...

You piss in the bushes and rub it into the ground with your shoe.

...

You hide.

...

It's quiet again.

...

People probably hate you.

That's up to them.

...

But they should hate you for the true reasons, not the bullshit in the paper.

...

Actually, you've no real interest in whether people love you or hate you. You could have some kids who think, yeah, you're the best thing since sliced bread because you're going around, you know, going to war with the police, out in the hills in Rothbury, and there are some kids who probably do want to put you on a T-shirt and have a fan club or something, that's what you read, but fuck that. And you could have other ones who are totally ignorant, who've been fed this crap in the newspapers, and they think you're this lunatic who stamped on Sam's belly, you know. For fuck's sake, that does piss you off. But this thing about going out in a blaze of glory, you couldn't give a fuck about that, because there's no prize here. There's no blaze of glory on the crags. Nothing fantastic is going to be achieved out of this. Your kids are going to be disgraced for the rest of their lives for what their father did. Sam's going to be disgraced for what you did. Six years with you, a fucking lunatic. All the people you care about are going to suffer through this. You can do what you can to make things right, but there's no blaze of glory.

...

You get up and look around. Nobody can see you.

...

You lie in the crevice. You could hide here until the cows come home and they won't find you, but at the end of the day you've got no food so something's got to happen. It's not like you can shoot a rabbit, not without them hearing, though if you could then you'd be fine, because you used to eat rabbit all the time when you were training properly. Rabbit curry. Rabbit pasta. Rabbit sandwiches. Rabbit and peas. Rabbit's an excellent source of protein and it was essential when you were huge, much bigger than you are now. You lost a lot of weight in the past few months particularly. You've not half lost a lot of weight. Part of that's jail, because you've got your meal times in there and they're pathetic. The food's fucking horrible, you know. You don't get enough of it. You get no protein. But a lot of it's the stress too, and also it's harder in the gym when you get older, like in the past few years you've just been lifting a few weights to keep yourself looking nice for Sam and kids, because the kids like their dad to be muscly, but nothing like when you were on the doors at your peak and looked the part. You really did. Women loved it. The problem is, to look like that you had to treat your body like a machine, and if you treat your body like a machine it'll break like a machine, so there were problems, like joints and tendons, and you lost an inch off your spine from doing ridiculous deadlifts, three hundred and fifty kilos. You're six-three now, but you used to be six-four, and it was deadlifts that took that extra height off. You were gutted when you found out, which is why you backed off from that a bit. Actually, one of the worst things was the hunger pains. One week you'd have eight thousand calories per day, then you'd read some research and drop down to a strict fifteen hundred calories per day, and it was permanent worrying about strength gains, because it's hard to get big. People think it isn't, but it is. It's easy to make gains of five per cent, little gains like that, but when you're powerlifting and bodybuilding you're going for seven per cent, preferably ten, and that's not easy, not at all. Not many guys can do what you did, and it was a constant puzzle, trying to make gains, trying to figure out why gains were stagnating, working out whether it was because of the movement restrictions of a particular machine, or if you weren't doing enough reps, or if you were tired from a lack of sleep or having sex the night before. You tried all kinds of things to keep the gains going. You tried Testosterone Cypionate [600mg per week], which was a black-market counterfeit version that didn't seem very effective. You tried Ephedrine. You tried Nandrolone Decanoate [600mg per week]. And what was interesting actually, was you found out you've got these high levels of natural testosterone, which explained a lot of the problems you experienced when experimenting with steroids [you wrote in your training diary in 1997 that it caused you extreme anti-social behaviour and personality changes]. The other problem was your liver. You had these blood tests that showed your liver was being overused, and that probably could have been the steroids, which is why you laid off it for periods, to cleanse your

132

system and allow hormonal functions to normalise. When you were off it you just used Creatine, to make sure the muscle didn't atrophy. The general public goes on about steroids, but they're a must for the classic bodybuilding ripped look. Unfortunately you always had problems with water retention, which decreased your definition, so you'd try different dietary intakes to fix that, and basically the perfect diet is forty per cent protein, thirty per cent carbs and thirty per cent fat, but the timing of food is crucial to prevent fat storage, and actually, you can also split it thirty-three per cent protein, thirty-three per cent carbs and thirty-three per cent fats, but anyway, you looked puffy sometimes, in the face especially, but you read about this Russian professor who had a theory that if you increased dietary fat you'd get more ripped, which you can remember having a bit of a reservation about, thinking it might increase your testosterone levels, which would mean temper tantrums and rage occurring off as well as on courses of steroids, and there'd be more stress on the liver and kidneys, but you gave it a serious try. The thing was though, a lot of the time these experiments just made you feel even more fatigued, or when you increased your fat intake it would make you look ripped, but there'd be a downside like a film of dietary fat over your body, which is why you'd experiment and try Gabba or Winstrol. Sometimes you worried it was making you ill, particularly if it was one you hadn't tried before. Like, you had flatulence and diarrhoea for a bit, or bloating, and at one point you suspected you had a digestive disorder. And you had this weird burning sensation behind your nipples, and hard lumps, which was a definite cause for concern, and that's why you switched to Sustanon [you weren't using steroids at the time of the shootings]. Still, there's not many guys that are twenty stone with abdominals, and it took a lot to get there. You weren't big when you were a kid. The opposite in fact. You were a skinny kid and you had these granddad glasses with elastic bits that went around your ears, which you hated, and you remember pretending you'd lost them, and you had this bright ginger hair, like a carrot top. Nothing like you were once you were on the doors. Obviously there was teasing about it when you were a kid, and you still get that sometimes, which isn't right, because you shouldn't tease people for being different, and actually, just recently you woke up in the middle of the night because someone was shouting something about there being a big ginger bastard, so you went to the door in your boxers, but whoever it was had legged it. You hated being skinny though. You used to pray to the little Jesus nailed to the wooden cross. Jesus the Saviour you called it. You prayed to be big, so you could look after yourself, and that's how you got into martial arts. You'd get the games imported from Japan, and you were into wrestling in your teens, which is why you had your hair like British Bulldog, and you had a hell of a talent for the martial arts. You did that for a lot of years, went semi-pro in cage fighting, could have taught it really, but that was when it first started, when you did it back home in France and in Crete, places like that. It hadn't really taken off over here at the time. This is going back about ten years. It's popular as hell now, but they've spoiled it as far as you're concerned. The principle behind it originally was to have any style against any style. It was fantastic then, when the basic disciplines were Muay Thai and grappling. You were a worry for other fighters because that's exactly what you did, but since then everyone's realised they're the two martial arts that win, so they're all doing it, and when you get in the ring now there's no advantages or disadvantages. It's like a game of chess. They still fight abroad with any style though, like in Crete, but they've killed it here, made it into a proper sport, which is why you lost interest. Also you picked up a lot of injuries, the worst was your right hip, from doing the splits all the time. Your party trick was putting two chairs out and straddling across the lot, but you started to feel the pain in there, especially when you were doing your side kicks, things like that, and you did exactly what you shouldn't, because you were busy working all over the country trying to earn a future, so you ignored it, and that was silly, thinking about it now, and it wasn't until years later that you went to the doctor and he said, look, it's not from training, it's genetic, but of course when you said you needed it replaced so you could get back into the cage-fighting, it didn't go down too well with the doctor, and you'd have had to get it done on private. But basically, the whole reason you got big was for the martial arts, and what happened was you got in the ring with this guy who was twenty-four or twenty-five stone, a big hay-maker, this bar-brawler type, with hair everywhere. You can still remember him now. You'd seen tape recordings of his fights, and you were worried to be honest, because he was monstrous, buckling guys with shots to the body. You'd never seen anything like it. But you took him down to the ground, and as you were going down he hit you and everything just went bong. His hands were as big as your head, big windmills coming in from all over the place, but you got him in a chokehold, so it worked for you obviously, but you could feel that difference in size when he hit you, and that's when you realised you needed to be bigger.

…

It's getting dark. The helicopter's gone.

…

You're hungry.

…

But stress makes you lose a lot of weight. It's happened before. You lost five stone once through stress. Another time you lost three stone, a few years ago, when you told the psychiatrist you had this feeling you might snap, and obviously that could be dangerous, because you're a big guy, and you'd been having these thoughts of smashing up a police car. When the police actually came to the house you almost did lose your temper. You picked up a loaded crossbow, though in fairness you put it down and discussed it with them, but clearly that's not right. And you were having all these symptoms, like your memory wasn't right, you couldn't concentrate for more than a paragraph, you had shortness of breath, sweating, pacing a lot and crying. You couldn't stop thinking about things people had done to you. You spent entire days angry about it, with these sensations in your head, and you were watching the CCTV

136

cameras all the time, thinking about suicide, which you tried when you were a teenager [you told people you took an overdose of medication as a teenager, and you were taken to hospital after taking a deliberate overdose of medication in 1999], but nobody would help [you'd been referred to the psychiatrist after seeing your GP and a mental health worker, and the psychiatrist referred you for psychotherapy, but you didn't show up for the two appointments you were given]. It was around then that you broke your hand and went to A&E. You told the doctor a heavy engine block had fallen on it, two hundred and fifty kilos, and the hand surgeon wanted you to stay in hospital because you were supposed to keep it raised, but you had too much going on with the family [that's what you told them]. You started having problems with your allergies again too, which was making your asthma worse, so you went to the GP and asked for the desensitisation treatment you had when you were younger, and the GP said the specialist wouldn't agree to it, but they referred you anyway [the GP wrote that he was referring you due to your insistence rather than his worries], and you went to the RVI [to the Department of Respiratory Medicine] where you told them that the bad asthma you had as a kid had come back, so they examined you and diagnosed you [the doctor wrote that you had moderate to severe asthma] and they said to come back for more tests [you were also referred for physiotherapy, but didn't show up]. You got Achilles tendonitis as well, which you needed an ultrasound for, and you were getting headaches [the GP gave you codeine]. Anyway, you went for the respiratory tests at the RVI [the doctor said you were well oxygenated, but had mild wheezing] and they wanted to give you a drug, but you weren't keen, because it had steroids in it and you'd seen this documentary about thinning bones and how steroids can speed it up, and actually, you'd been able to feel your bones getting thinner and weaker, so you told them you were worried about that because you'd been using your steroid inhaler since you were a kid. They said inhalers are fine, so you had to insist, look, you need a bone mineral density scan and you also want the desensitisation treatment for your allergies [the doctor noted that you said you were happy to accept any risk, including death], but they still wouldn't give you the bone scan. It doesn't matter now. Anyway, you got your skin tested [at the Immunology Department] and they realised you're allergic to dust mites and cats and dogs, so you started treatment [they said it might not work as well as it did when you were younger] and then you had to go back to hospital because they thought you were inhaling too much corticosteroid, and what they did was split the medicine into two parts and told you to come back in three months [you didn't attend the follow-up appointment or another scheduled test]. It was around then that your bicep became painful as well, so you went to see the GP about that [and while you were there you said English is your second language and mentioned you were having relationship problems]. Then you went to the GP again and said the police and the council were victimising you, so they referred you to a counsellor [the GP wrote that you might benefit from anger management], but you didn't show up for the first session. You were missing appointments all over the place by then, due to the stress with the police and everything else going on [you didn't show up for the second counselling session, or the third, but you showed up for a few after that, then missed a few, then went to one, then missed a couple, then turned up for a few], but in the end what happened is you went to jail so obviously the counselling stopped [you told the prison staff you needed your allergy medicine, which they got for you from the RVI, and you also asked for eczema medicine for your back, and a chlamydia check].

…

It's night-time. You're cold. You pull your hoodie up.

…

It's pitch dark. You pace backwards and forwards.

…

You hide.

…

But being big worked against you with the social workers, because they were witches [there is no evidence that any social workers did anything wrong], writing you off as aggressive. In fairness, you're an imposing man, intimidating, you can't help that, and you told them that, but they put it down in this report, saying you'd intimidated them, and when it came up at one of the meetings you told them at no point did you take steps towards them or raise your hands or raise your voice or anything like that. Definitely. At no point did you threaten anybody. And if this social worker did feel intimidated, well that's purely down to them. You found things like that offensive, to be honest, and what actually happened was the social worker was arguing the case, and you being you, and this was never intended as a threat, but you asked this totally rhetorical question, and it was clear you were just pointing out the ridiculousness of it all, but in it went, into the report, saying how you'd threatened them, and it got brought up in this meeting, so you told them, look, English is your second language, and fair enough, you speak it very well, but it's still a second language for you, and you'd been worried that this could happen, because sometimes you do say things that get misinterpreted. But anyway, they asked you what you thought the solution to all this was and you told them how you just wanted to draw a line under everything, because if you kept fighting them they'd keep fighting back, and you knew you were going to lose, one hundred per cent, because it was a conspiracy, the charge was a conspiracy, so you told them that all you wanted was a psychiatrist or a psychologist, someone to have a word with you on a regular basis to find out whether there was an underlying problem you hadn't seen, because it's easy for you to say there's nothing wrong, but you needed a professional, not a DIY thing, to come along and say what the problem is and what can be improved, someone to sit down with you, just in case, because they wanted to hang you from the highest height, and fucking hell, you can't believe they've had you in jail over this, which is partly why you're so pissed off, because you didn't deserve to get fucked over, you tried your best, you did everything right, you worked hard and did what society wanted, and what did they do? They turned you into an ogre who lives under a bridge and eats goats.

YOU WILL DIE TOMORROW

Right, this is it. No it isn't. Fuck it. You can easily kill yourself. Killing yourself's not a fucking problem, it'll be very fucking easy, but you're not ready yet. You stay hidden.

…

It's warm today.

…

You cover yourself with bits of trees and leaves. You've found a little spot in the woods. There's nobody around. You hide.

…

Maybe they've stopped visitors coming up. Usually there are loads of visitors coming up here [you're at a National Trust site called Cragside], but there's nobody around, so maybe they've stopped visitors. You get up and walk to a split in the trees. You

143

look down the track and walk along it. You leave the phone on a bridge. You go back. Lie down. These last few days have really taken the stuffing out of you. You can't stop thinking about Sam. You put leaves on your legs. Because you tried so hard to fix things, but you got nowhere, and she pushed too far. Maybe now she understands the effect that her being like that had on you, but yes, you definitely made mistakes. That's fair. You're not perfect, you know that. But it was the nastiness and hurtful words that did this to you. Maybe deep down she wanted this. That's what you keep thinking. You wish you could talk to her. You miss her. She was the only one who understood what was happening. That's the thing, anybody who knows you, they know you've stood on the doors in front of kids who are drugged up and kids who are drunk, kids calling you, kids calling your kids, kids calling your mum, provoking you in every way, and you've handled that, looked after yourself there, but the fact is, these idiots believed these allegations, and now it's ended up here. All this because of a piffling Section 39 [an assault on a child]. You could have put your hands up to it from the start and told a lie and said, look, sorry, it's the steroids, it's the smack, you know, and got a pat on the back and an ahhh we'll help you, but you fought it, you know, and now a Section 39 has come to a multiple murder. It's emotional abuse, being honest. The police emotionally abused you. They made you not well. People think you're happy, but you know from yourself you're not. At the Collingwood [where you saw the psychiatrist] they said you're fine, that your main problem is acceptance, because you were rejected by your mum, and your dad is over in France, and fair enough, you were passed from pillar to post, but you've managed to bring yourself up well with a high sense of morals. And even though you were dragged up, you know the difference between right and wrong, but thinking about it, maybe your childhood did affect you as a dad, because your experience was a handbook of how not to bring kids up. Maybe that had a positive impact.

...

A dog comes through the bushes. It looks at you. It doesn't bark. You stay still. It goes away.

...

You go to the stream and drink. You splash your face.

...

You lie in a patch of heather and dry in the sunshine.

...

You go to your new hiding spot.

...

You still have these nightmares where you're seven years old and chased by monsters. You're not well. Your mum wasn't well. She used to say weird things, and your gran [who you

145

lived with when you were little], she said your mum wasn't well. You loved your gran though. She was the most important person in the world to you. Her and Sam. But when your mum married Brian, that's when you and Angus had to leave gran's and move in with them, and it was like butter wouldn't melt with Brian [your mum told a reporter that you hated Brian; Angus got on with him]. And since then you've talked to your mum probably once in the last fifteen years and it was most unpleasant, which is why you're massively estranged from your family, though your cousin did get in touch not long ago saying she'd been asked by your Auntie Barbara [your mum's sister] to find you and Angus, and it was quite touching to be honest [it made you cry]. There was you thinking nobody wanted anything to do with you, but shortly after that, Barbara died, and your mum didn't even go to the funeral, her own sister, so think about that. But you went, and when you were there you showed them photos of the kids and stuff, and told them about the business. Even that was a problem for the council though, because you called them up and said you couldn't make a meeting because of the funeral. You just wanted to check it wouldn't jeopardise the deal. What it was is, you'd made this deal that you'd turn up for five meetings on time without missing one, because they had a bee in their bonnet about you being late. So you said to her on the phone that there was this funeral coming up, and you'd never had anything to do with your English family for twenty years and didn't think you'd be welcome after cutting them off for a lot of reasons, but this side of the family still wanted you to go, and you did get on with these particular members, but the thing is, it's

146

not part of your culture to show huge disrespect by watching someone get chucked in the ground then shooting off, so you needed to go for a decent amount of time, which is why you told this woman how you couldn't make the session, but also you didn't want to jeopardise this deal, and suddenly she was saying it was beyond her jurisdiction [your word] to make a deal like that [on a recording, made by you, a social worker does set you a target of attending five meetings without being late or cancelling, but the reward for achieving that target isn't clarified] and what you realised was, this was all just part of the Get Raoul Moat brigade. It's why you started using the tapes, so you could pull them, and they hated you using the tapes. When you told them you were recording everything they started going on about their human rights. What about your human rights? You should have taken all the recordings to the press and blown them away, but it was typical of the way they carried on, never giving you any light at the end of the tunnel.

[There is no evidence that the council did anything wrong.]

...

You walk along the riverbank in Rothbury. The main street is a hundred metres away. You eat peppers and tomatoes from an allotment. You hide behind a wall. People see you.

...

You walk along a street in Rothbury. People see you.

…

You hide.

…

Gran's probably looking down wishing you'd stop all this, and being honest, you do miss her. She was special to you, with her tiny hands and feet, looking after you, even when you moved in with Brian and your mum, she'd still look after you, living round the corner, and you used to go over and help her out, and she'd give you dinner, things like that, but she wasn't half frail, deaf as a plank by then too. She used to turn her TV up so loud that the neighbours would complain about migraines and daft things like that, knocking on the door of this poor old deaf lady. They even called the cops one time, but when the cops got there they said the volume on the TV was fine and they just gave the neighbours a bollocking for wasting police time. They even started knocking on the wall when you went round to do the hoovering one time, so you just picked the hoover up and hoovered the wall, probably did that for ten minutes, which drove the point home, you know, ha ha. Anyway, she got so frail she couldn't even turn on the microwave, so she got put in a home and you'd visit her there too, but she died. To all intents your gran raised you. She used to keep track of immunisations and things like that, take you all over for days out. One time, and you remember this clearly, she took you and Angus to Tynemouth and you found these inner tubes from a car on the beach so you went out to sea on them, miles out, and Gran was back on the beach, going off it, shouting about calling the coastguard. Looking back, it was dangerous, to be fair, a bit scary for her probably, because if the tide had been going out you would have been knackered. But you just jumped off and swam back and climbed up these rusty ladders. You and Angus were both good swimmers. Some people didn't like Gran, but that was just because she was honest, like you are. If she found anything wrong with you she'd tell you, and even though she was tiny, she wouldn't be stepped on, not by anybody. Some people called her a man-hater, and fair enough, she didn't like a lot of men very much, but she doted on you and Angus. It was just independence really, because there was never a man around. Your granddad wasn't around, though you're named after him [he was called Thomas Hall Moat and Thomas is your middle name]. Nobody talked about him. You've only ever seen pictures of him in a photo album made from giraffe hide from World War Two. He was a champion boxer in the army in North Africa, and after the war him and Gran moved to Canada with your mum and aunties, but your gran thought he was dangerous, because one time she was stood on the edge of a cliff with him and she thought he was going to push her off, so she packed her bags and came back to Newcastle with the girls. Nobody ever heard from him again.

...

There's a fighter jet flying over.

...

You eat a mouse, but you might be dreaming.

YOU WILL DIE TODAY

You crawl out of base camp.

...

It's 10.30am. You walk along the riverbank, past the nice houses that overlook the river in Rothbury. People see you.

...

You wash in the river.

...

You hide.

...

A helicopter flies overhead.

...

A jet flies overhead.

...

You want this to be over.

...

You hide.

...

[The police don't know how you spent your time while hiding.]

...

It's 7pm. You walk past the nice houses overlooking the river again and there's a man and a woman walking across the stepping-stones so you stand behind a tree. You watch them. The woman looks at you. She nods and you look at her, but you don't respond.

DROP YOUR WEAPON!!!

The shout comes from behind.

You turn around.

It's over.

There's a cop with his face pressed to the sight of his gun, and he's got a helmet on and body armour on and his gun pointing at you, and if you point your gun at them it's over.

…

…

You point your gun at your right temple and shout,

Shoot me fucking shoot me.

He's saying put your weapon down, put your weapon down, but you don't, and you start walking to your left, toward the little fence, and he's following you and saying stand still, stand still.

You stand still.

He shouts,

Get down on the floor.

You kneel on the grass.

He shouts,

Think of the girls.

You tell him the police have had everything off you. They wouldn't leave you alone. And he says they don't know you, they're not from here, they're from Yorkshire, and you tell him you can hear their accents, and you calm down, and your voice gets quieter.

You lie on your stomach.

Your baseball cap is pulled low.

You keep the gun pointed at your head. The river is behind you, and the police are in front of you. More police keep arriving. More guns keep pointing at you. A car to the left has police around it, cars to the right have police around them, and there's probably some behind you for an ambush, there'll have to be an ambush, and you'll shoot yourself when the ambush comes, so you wait.

…

The negotiators arrive. They come to the edge of the grass, to where the first officers are standing. They crouch behind ballistic shields. They don't have helmets. You can see their hands and heads over the top of the shields. One of them shouts,

Raoul, my name's _____, alright. I'm here to help you. Nobody is going to hurt you while you're talking to me, right.

You listen. He keeps talking,

The most important thing is that we don't want you to hurt yourself either. Can you hear me alright?

He carries on,

Right, Raoul, you have got a future. You have got a future.

You're lying.

He shouts back,

What, sorry, Raoul? I'm not lying to you, Raoul. I'm not lying to you. Do you want me to tell you how you've got a future, Raoul?

You tell him you can't do the jail. He says,

Raoul, Raoul, in twenty years' time you'll still only be fifty-seven, Raoul. You're still a young man. You're a fit man.

He says this is your chance to tell the world what happened, so you should put the gun down and talk to him.

You won't.

He says there'll be an independent investigation and they'll look at everything that's happened.

157

Too late for that.

He says it's not too late.

You tell him nobody cares about you, and he says everybody cares about you, he cares about you, these officers care about you, your daughters care about you, but the helicopter's too loud to hear properly, so you tell him to come closer, and he says,

Raoul, Raoul, I will come closer, and listen to me when I say this because this is very, very, very important. I will come closer if you put that gun down, alright?

But you won't, and he stays where he is and talks about your kids.

I haven't gained their respect.

He can't hear you, so he says they'll move forward, and they move forward, and he thanks you. He says you need to come in so you can tell your daughters what happened. He asks how long you were in jail and you tell him. You talk about jail and your daughters.

...

...

There's someone behind you.

…

He says there's nobody behind you.

There is. You can hear them.

There's nobody behind you, Raoul.

There is. You can hear them. They're in the bush.

Raoul, there's nobody in the bush.

There's definitely somebody in the bush now.

Raoul, listen to me — nobody will hurt you while you're talking to me. As long as we're talking to each other, you will not be hurt.

Definitely someone behind me.

Raoul, there is nobody.

I can see people from behind.

And he keeps telling you there's nobody there, just a river.

I can hear them.

He says it might be the birds in the trees.

It's not the birds.

He says nobody's going to hurt you and asks if you believe him.

No, I don't.

He says he wouldn't be here if they were going to hurt you.

You answer him [most of your answers aren't recorded as the negotiator's dictaphone is too far away from you]. He says,

Raoul, I know that you're a logical thinker, you're an intelligent man. I've seen that from your letters.

…

He stops talking.

…

He starts again,

Raoul, what you can hear is a group of kids in the field. I've just seen them. There's one with a stripy top on. They're in a garden at the back. Can you hear the kids shouting? That's what you can hear, Raoul. I've just looked up and seen them. That's what you can hear. Okay, Raoul? That's what you can hear. It doesn't sound like a man's voice, does it? It sounds like kids. Listen to the voices. It's kids. That's all it is, Raoul. That's what you can hear. Now listen, I apologise for not hearing that, and not seeing that, and you did. Now I'm sorry for that. Listen to me, Raoul, ignore them. Ignore them. You're the most important thing.

He asks if you still trust him. You answer.

He says they're moving the kids away.

…

He says he knows you're intelligent and articulate and that you're not an idiot. He says he knows you think everything through. He says he wants you to tell him about the real Raoul Moat.

You answer.

He can't hear. He asks you to lift your head. You shout,

Sam and the kids.

Sam and the kids?

All I care about.

You tell him you tried to be a good dad, but the police bullied you. He says it'll all come out in the inquiry.

You tell him you've provided for Sam. He says you're right.

I couldn't do it any other way.

He says you need to be a dad.

It's too late for that.

…

He asks about the conviction and Mr Trimmit.

You keep answering. He says you don't know the future.

I do.

He asks what you want to be.

A normal guy.

You are a normal guy, Raoul.

I'm not.

…

Raoul, please can you do me another favour, when you move

162

about with that, please be careful with that gun, will you?

…

You hear something again.

He says they'll close the path off so nobody else can get behind there. He asks you to put the gun down.

I'm not putting it down.

…

He talks about your kids and the future and says you shouldn't jeopardise that.

It's already gone.

It hasn't.

Nobody can tell me what's the matter with me.

…

You tell him nobody gave you a chance. He says,

Raoul, Raoul, Raoul, look at me. Raoul, look at me. I'm giving you that chance now. I'm giving you that escape route.

It's too late for that.

Raoul, tomorrow is a new day.

It's not.

…

He says all police aren't the same, just like everybody in the legal system isn't the same, and just like everybody in the council isn't the same. There's good and bad in everything.

I know that.

He says the girls need you.

You know I'm not coming in.

He asks if you want to live to tell the girls how the world works.

No, I don't.

He asks if you planned it to be like this.

No, I didn't plan it to be like this.

He says this isn't the end, it's the beginning,

The moment you put that gun down and walk over here to be

with me, it's a new start for you. Listen, the hardest part of this, the hardest part of this is making that first step now, Raoul.

Do you know what the hardest part of this has been?

What?

I miss her.

You miss Sam?

Yeah.

I don't doubt for one minute that you miss Sam, and I know that you love her deeply.

Which is why I can't come in.

Of course you can.

I can't, I can't, I can't.

…

Your head drops. He asks you to look up.

…

He says he's read your letters. He says you're a dignified man.

...

He asks if you'll move the gun a tiny bit away from your head.

No.

...

He asks if you're thirsty.

Very.

He asks if you want something to eat. You do.

He asks what kind of sandwich you'd like.

Anything.

Anything?

Anything, anything.

He says he'll try to get food, but you're holding a shotgun.

I won't hurt anyone.

He believes you. He's not sure how to get a sandwich to you.

Chuck it at me.

Chuck it at you?

Yeah.

He says they'll try, but he can't promise.

...

He says all police aren't the same and you answer him [your answer isn't recorded by the dictaphone]. He says,

You see, Raoul. You don't. You've decided, you've made that decision, because you're an educated man, that enough people have been hurt. I know what you said before, that all you wanted was a straightener for this lad, but you do know he wasn't a police officer, don't you?

Is that the truth?

Raoul, that is the truth.

You tell him the police made the guy out to be a hero, but he says they didn't make anyone out to be heroes. He tells you,

Raoul, he was a karate instructor. He was a karate instructor.

Is that all he was? Awwww.

Yes, listen, Raoul, look at me. Look at me, Raoul, Raoul, Raoul.

You don't respond.

...

He says,

Raoul, mistakes happen. You acted on the information that you were given by somebody who you love.

He says it's not your fault.

You say you don't understand why she did it.

He says it's not your fault.

He asks you to put the gun down.

I'm not coming in. Seriously, listen, I'm not coming in.

...

You tell him you don't understand why she lied. He says,

Raoul, Raoul, Raoul.

You talk about Sam.

...

You want to sit up. He says you can. He asks about the safety.

It's off.

The safety's off?

The safety's off.

You start sitting up. He wants you to keep talking, keep facing him, be careful, get comfortable. You sit on your bum.

…

You talk about Sam and compensation, and what's been in the papers, and the violence. There's no point in coming in.

He says you're back to the beginning. He says you should come in and have a bite to eat, get something to drink, have a shower, a shave, get a change of clothes, so the real Raoul Moat can appear.

You respond, and he asks what brought you here to this river-bank.

I'd just had enough.

…

He says in ten years, twenty years, thirty years, you could

meet someone else, not another Sam, there's only one Sam, but someone.

You tell him she was the one. He says everyone gets a second or third or fourth or fifth chance to find their happiness.

I don't want to find anybody else.

You don't want to?

No.

…

He says things will change, starting when you put the gun down.

I cannot do the jail.

He says you'll have support.

You talk about your kids.

You talk about Sam.

You ask again,

Was he not in the police?

He swears it's the truth. He says you've been misled. You tell him it'll be covered up again. He says it won't.

I cannot spend the rest of my life in jail.

He says,

You'll not be. I don't know what sentence you'll get for what's happened, Raoul, be a long one, not going to lie to you. It'll be a long sentence, but you haven't got a lot of previous, have you?

No, that was my only one.

Exactly.

But you tell him you'll get a maximum sentence because you shot a police officer.

He says he doesn't know what you'll get, but it's not as dark as you might be thinking. There is a future. Put the gun down.

You don't.

…

You ask if a psychologist has been involved. He says there has been, and what the psychologist said was that you're educated and have strong morals and you respect people, and you're not nuts.

I've got to be nuts for doing this.

He says you're not, you're not.

You tell him you've been like this for a month. He says it's the stress. You tell him they gave you drugs in jail and it made you numb, but they've worn off now and you've settled down.

I'm not coming in.

He says he can see you've settled down, but can you put the gun on your knee? You won't. He says nobody will rugby-tackle you.

If I put it down you will hit me in the shoulder.

Raoul, this works on trust and respect. I've told you.

It will give you an opportunity.

He says you can put the gun down then pick it back up.

You don't.

He says nobody will shoot you.

You tell him you're not going to do anything bad to them.

He says he believes you.

He asks about sleep and says he doesn't want you to fall asleep.

I'm not going to fall asleep.

He doesn't want you to faint.

Well I have fainted today.

Right, now I'm worried. You're telling me that you fainted today, you've been on medication historically that could, that should be out your system, but you don't know.

You tell him you're okay.

He says if you come in you can have a shower and food, and the police will investigate everything.

You answer him.

You talk about the conviction.

He says the police will have to look at that.

Well I got found guilty.

That's not right, is it?

No.

He says you'll get a chance to explain.

You tell him it's done. You tell him they'll cover it up.

He says they wouldn't dare.

He says you can tell the world you are the real Raoul Moat.

I'm still going to be away from Sam.

He goes through it all again. Sam, kids, the future.

You talk about your gran and how much you loved her.

You talk about prison and your children.

Will they forgive me for what I've done?

…

…

He talks about Sam. You respond.

He says he knows you've been wrongly done to.

Do you believe that?

He says he does.

...

He explains what will happen with the food. He tells you three officers are going to come from your left. Two of them will be carrying shields. The third will have the food. That officer will put the food down, about ten feet away from where you're sitting, and you mustn't move until they've retreated.

He asks you to repeat what will happen. You repeat it.

He tells you again what will happen and asks what you can't do.

Go for the food when they're there.

...

The midges are in your face. You knock them away.

He says you should come in and get something to eat, get your sugar levels up and tell everyone what happened.

You answer.

He says,

Raoul, while you're talking to me I've said to you, no one is going to hurt you. We want you, everyone here wants you, to put the gun down and just walk and just come to us and that's it. The midges will be gone, you can get more food, you can have a shower, a shave and everything squared off. I mean, like I say, you've asked for the kids to be moved, we moved the kids out the back who you thought were cops. They weren't. We've done everything that you've asked of us, Raoul. We moved to here. There were no tricks there. Will you at least, when you've had your food, do that for me?

I'll think about it.

Thank you.

But I'm not promising anything.

I know. Thank you.

…

You tell him you want to apologise to the people of Rothbury. He says you don't need to.

It's getting dark. He says they'll set up some lights.

…

You ask where he's from. He says,

You've got South Yorkshire, West Yorkshire, Cleveland, Durham, Humberside. They're from all over.

176

You tell him you've heard all kinds of accents. He says you must have been close to them. You tell him you were.

...

He says it'll be an all-day breakfast sandwich.

There'll be a big bottle of water too.

You ask how Sam is. He says she's a lot better.

You ask about the injury. He describes it.

The food's ready.

He says they'll throw it to you. They'll have their guns drawn, but they won't be pointed at you.

You knock some midges away.

They bring the food towards you.

They get close.

One throws the sandwich. Then the water.

It rolls, but you grab it.

They retreat. You ask,

How much do you get paid for this?

...

As you unwrap the sandwich you keep the gun under your chin and he says,

Raoul. Raoul. Whoa, whoa. Be careful. Just watch where you're putting your hand. Why don't you just put the gun by your foot?

You won't. He asks if you want peace while you eat.

No, no, it's not that.

He stops talking. You eat the sandwich. It's a triple.

...

You talk to him about calming down this week. He says,

Yes. You obviously took the right decision though, Raoul. You made the right decision. I mean, you had the chance to hurt another officer and you didn't.

He asks what you've been doing for water. You tell him.

He says that can give you a bad gut.

He says you've got a future.

How's the officer?

He says he won't die, but he's lost the sight in one eye, but not the other, and he's been promised he can keep his job.

You ask a question about the officer. He says he doesn't know and that he only knows the stuff in the press. He tries talking about you instead.

You ask another question about the officer. He says he'll be looked after the same as you will be and he tries talking about something else.

You ask who the officer was. He says PC Rathband.

You tell him you're worried Sam is in trouble. He says she's not.

...

You thank them for the food. He says you're welcome.

He says you should have a drink of water, then put your gun down and walk up the road with him to get a couple of sandwiches.

You won't.

...

You ask about Sam. You talk about her dad.

You talk about Sam and you.

It's getting dark. He asks if you'll put the gun down.

No.

...

He says they'll put the lights up, but he really wants you to put the gun down. You won't. Fair enough, there's no rush.

You ask about Sam and Chris. He says he doesn't know anything about their relationship.

He asks if it's okay to turn the lights of the Mitsubishi on. It's fine. And the BMW? It's fine. You knock the midges. He says,

Raoul, you alright? Sick of the midges? Listen, Raoul, where's that, where's that, I cannot see the gun. Where is it?

He wants you to be careful.

I'm not coming in.

Why not?

You tell him you're wasting his time.

He says you're not, he says the kids need a dad, whether it's in ten years' or twenty years' time.

He says the car engines need to go on before they can switch the headlights on. You tell him it's fine.

They turn the headlights on.

He talks about your future again. You talk about being a dad and being in jail and the shootings. You tell him you don't want to waste taxpayers' money. He says you can't put a price on life.

He asks when you last slept. You tell him you've had catnaps.

He asks what brought you down today. You tell him you were tired.

He says you must feel lonely. You tell him you do get lonely.

You talk about it all. Again. Again. Again.

He talks about your future. Again and again.

He says everything will be better after a good night's sleep.

You tell him you need to speak to Sam.

He says she's in hospital.

You tell him only Sam can sort this out.

You ask about Karl and Sean. He says he doesn't know what's happened with them. You tell him they were hostages.

You talk about the kids.

They set up some more lights.

He asks about you and Sam. You talk about her.

He says,

She hasn't got all the answers, mate.

…

He says you need to stick around for the kids. He says you can get help. You talk about jail. He says you can get help in jail.

You're getting quiet.

…

They're putting lights up on the other side of the river.

He asks you to put the gun down.

You won't.

You tell him you want to speak to Sam. He says you can't.

He says you need to look forward, not back.

You ask if Sam's said she doesn't want to speak to you.

He says,

No, Sam's in hospital. She isn't very well, but she will get better. It's not … Raoul, if she said that she didn't want to speak to you, I'd tell you that she didn't want to speak to you, but that isn't the case. It's because she's in hospital. You need, if you love her, you need to give her the chance to get better and then speak to her.

He talks about the kids. He asks you to put the gun down.

You're worried about what people will say to the kids.

He says they'll be fine.

He says,

What's stopping you, when you come out, emigrating and your kids coming with you? Or moving to a different part of the country?

He says there are places like Rothbury all over. He says you can build a new life, starting from now.

You tell him you can't.

He says you've been through all this already, you've got to listen, because he's solving the problems you're raising.

…

He talks about your kids.

He says he knows you're getting sleepy.

He asks you to put the gun down.

You tell him they'll get you. He says they won't.

He says he does this because he cares about people, whether it's someone on a bridge or someone in a situation like this.

You ask if he's married.

You ask what your mum said to the papers. He doesn't know.

You talk about your mum. He talks about you and the kids.

You tell him you'll never get out of jail. He says you will.

He says it's in the press loads about how a life sentence doesn't really mean a life sentence.

You disagree.

He asks when the last time you saw a sentence like that was, because terrorists don't even get sentences like that.

You disagree.

He says you're jumping ahead, making assumptions, because you've hardly got any previous.

You tell him he's wrong.

…

He asks if you know anyone whose mum or dad committed suicide. You don't. He says it leaves an emptiness. He asks,

Have you thought about that, Raoul?

It starts raining.

You've been talking for hours.

You tell them you buried another gun at Cragside and you don't want any kids to find it. They could hurt themselves.

...

You're quiet.

...

You ask whether you're going to be able to speak to Sam on the phone. He says she would have to agree, and it would depend on logistics, and will you promise not to kill yourself?

You tell him no, and there's no point anyway because she probably wouldn't want to speak to you and you couldn't trust her.

He says you're moving the goalposts.

You tell him,

It ends in this field tonight.

You sit up straight, breathe deeply and move the gun from your chin to your head.

He shouts,

Look at me, look at me. No. Stop. Put the gun down.

Something hits your arm and knocks you backwards. You yelp, sit up straight, breathe deeply and shoot your head.

[DEAD]

Blood sprays out the left side of your head.

Your body falls backwards into the long grass.

Someone shouts,

Shots fired!

They come over to you.

Someone shouts,

Get the gun off him!

The gun's still in your left hand. They move it away.

Someone shouts,

Clear!

They pull you from the long grass. Your eyes are open.

Your eyeballs have rolled backwards.

Blood is pooled around your head and splattered across your face.

You're moaning.

They shout for a paramedic.

The paramedic runs over. You take a deep breath. He can't find the wound. He asks the police where you were shot and one of them gestures to the side of your head and they bring a light. The paramedic pulls your cap and hoodie out the way and sees the wound. They put a mask on your face and a defibrillator on your chest and an IV in your leg. They dress the hole in your head.

Your pulse is strong.

You're not breathing.

At 1.29am you leave Rothbury in an ambulance. They drive you through the countryside. The weather's bad. A convoy of police cars comes with you. They take you to a hospital in Newcastle, half an hour away. The doctors and nurses are waiting.

They take you out of the ambulance.

You're on a trolley.

They take you inside.

Something is hanging from your hoodie with wires attached. A nurse cuts it away. There are three shotgun cartridges in your pocket.

The nurse removes them. A metal ball falls to the floor from your pocket. She leaves it for the police.

You have a non-survivable shotgun wound to the head.

It's 2.16am. You're dead.

...

At 2.30am a chief inspector at a police station in Jarrow starts gathering initial accounts from officers who were there during the stand-off. Only three officers choose to provide accounts. Their solicitor reads out the accounts on their behalf.

The first,

I was the bronze commander at the scene. I briefed the officers on the parameters given to me by silver support prior to deployment. This included the independent use of less lethal options should the subject indicate that he intended to commit suicide. These options included the use of the X12 weapon.

The second,

In accordance with the set parameters I discharged the X12 because I believed he was trying to commit suicide as he put his gun to his head.

The third,

In accordance with the set parameters I discharged the X12 because I believed he was trying to commit suicide as he put his gun to his head.

The Independent Police Complaints Commission [IPCC] begins an investigation into the stand-off [in their subsequent report they describe the initial accounts as scant].

…

Northumbria Police announce that they fired tasers at you.

…

At 5pm on Saturday a pathologist cuts you open. Investigators from the IPCC watch. There is soot on the right side of your skull.

…

Two days later your uncle identifies your body.

...

On Tuesday July 13 a Northumbria Police officer finds a projectile on the riverbed in Rothbury. Police officers also look for the gun you said you left near a tree at Cragside. They find the location you described in detail, but there's no gun.

...

People leave flowers and notes at your house and at the riverbank in Rothbury. One of the notes says,

RIP Raoul. You were not helped and failed by the system massively.

...

On July 14 Prime Minister David Cameron tells Parliament,

As far as I can see it is absolutely clear that Raoul Moat was a callous murderer, full stop, end of story, and I cannot understand any wave, however small, of public sympathy for this man. There should be sympathy for his victims and for the havoc he wreaked in that community. There should be no sympathy for him.

...

On July 21 a second post-mortem is carried out by a different pathologist. Both examinations find abrasions on your body from living rough in Rothbury, an entry wound on the right side of your head, an exit wound on the left side, a complex skull fracture and extensive brain injury. There is also a U-shaped abrasion and bruise on the lower part of your arm which is consistent with a tangential blow from a taser projectile. They can't tell if it emitted a charge. You died from a shotgun wound to the head.

...

Angus and your friends empty your house. There are kids' toys in the garden. Computer games have dust on them. There are recordings of meetings with police and the council on your laptop. In the loft are stacks of videotapes containing footage you recorded with your CCTV cameras. There are piles of paperwork, including Mr Trimmit flyers [*If you've got it I'll Trimmit*] and lots of bills. One bill is from Littlewoods. The amount owed is £1075.12, which includes a debt-collection fee. It says court proceedings will start if the minimum payment of £322.20 is not made promptly. There's a letter from Your Homes Newcastle. You owe them £52.08. There's a letter from Newcastle City Council saying you have to repay £723.76 in overpaid benefit. There's a council tax bill. There's a renewal quote from your insurance company. There's a fine for £250.84 because you didn't have the correct vehicle licence. It includes a £60 charge for not paying on time and a note saying you'll have to pay in full within ten days or go to court and the fine will increase. There's a bank statement from March that says you had £47.52 in your account. There's a discharge letter from prison saying you received a grant of £46. There are letters about housing benefit, child benefit, child tax credit and working tax credit, and there's a letter saying your application for incapacity benefit was rejected. There's a letter from Your Homes Newcastle saying you've got three dogs, but your tenancy only permits one. There's a letter from Your Homes Newcastle saying you need to remove the ramp you built. There's a letter from Your Homes Newcastle saying they're removing the ramp you built and you're going to be charged for its removal. There's a letter from the police that is dated July 22 2009 and says,

It has been reported that you on Factory Road, Gateshead, on 2nd March, 2009, did commit the following offence:

NO INSURANCE — USE

The letter says they're dealing with the offence by issuing this written advice, but if you commit offences in the future then proceedings may be considered against you. This was the time you were pulled over by PC 190 [David Rathband] and they found copper piping and an old radiator in the vehicle, along with garden waste. They called an insurance bureau, who said you weren't insured to transport scrap metal, so they interviewed you under caution in the back of the police car and a recovery truck took your vehicle away [David Rathband wrote in his book that he had taken an instant disliking to you and wanted to seize your vehicle, but his colleague didn't, so he called a supervisor who agreed they should seize it]. You had to pay a release fee of £150, and £12 for each day of storage. A friend drove you home.

...

On August 2 you're cremated at the West Road Crematorium in Fenham. Angus is there. Your uncle is there. Friends are there.

...

On August 12 samples of your blood and urine are sent to the Home Office. A toxicologist examines them and decides you were not affected by drugs or alcohol when you died.

...

In March 2011 Karl and Sean go on trial at Newcastle Crown Court. Witnesses include Sam [who has recovered from her injuries] and David Rathband [who is permanently blinded]. Chris Brown's mum is in the public gallery. The jury decides Karl and Sean are guilty of conspiring to murder police officers, attempting to murder PC Rathband, and of robbing Mr Lehmer Singh. The jury also finds Karl guilty of murdering Chris Brown and possessing a gun with the intention of endangering life. Sean gets a minimum of twenty years in prison. Karl gets a minimum of forty years in prison.

...

Scott Raisbeck is sentenced to fifteen months in prison for moving the van, which was stolen from Hartlepool Borough Council.

...

In June 2011 the IPCC produces a report about the night you shot yourself. It criticises the openness of officers involved,

The process of obtaining witness statements, particularly from firearms officers and principal police officers performing the role of negotiators, was problematic and extremely protracted. The IPCC were not afforded direct access to these witnesses and all communication was directed through Police Federation Representatives and Counsel. In light of this and in an effort to gather witness evidence, statements were requested at an early stage of the investigation but were not provided until early in 2011. The evidence that they provided was considered as essential to the progression of the IPCC independent investigation. On receipt of the witness statements from the police negotiators, the content was found to be inadequate in assisting investigators in their understanding of the negotiators' role, what they witnessed and any decision making during the incident. The IPCC requested further witness statements from these police officers who did, with the exception of _____, provide further detail.

The report includes comment from a detective chief inspector who criticises the negotiators' use of a handheld digital dicta-phone because it produced poor-quality sound and was too far away from you to record most of what you said. It also stopped recording an hour and a half before you shot yourself.

Also in the report is contribution from the Home Office's taser expert. He describes the X12 taser as a shotgun that fires self-contained projectiles, giving it a longer range than normal tasers. When it hits a person, four prongs are supposed to penetrate the skin and produce an electrical charge. He says there is insufficient data to judge its safety and effectiveness. From post-mortem photographs of your body he believes a projectile hit your arm, but the prongs may not have penetrated the skin far enough to catch hold, possibly due to your thick hoodie.

The report says the Home Office had not approved the X12 or its projectiles. In the days before you died Northumbria Police were approached by Peter Boatman, a former police officer who became a director of Pro-Tect, which imported the X12. He delivered X12 shotguns and projectiles to Northumbria Police. Senior officers decided to use them despite knowing they were not approved. After your death the Home Office revoked Pro-Tect's licence, and three days later Peter Boatman died due to inhaling carbon monoxide. He had been in a shed with a lawnmower running while the door was closed. The coroner recorded an open verdict.

[The IPCC found no evidence of misconduct by any police officers involved in the stand-off.]

...

198

David Rathband's book, *Tango 190*, is published in July 2011. In a section about plans for a legal claim against Northumbria Police, he says,

What frightened me the most was that the information was being concealed. Tapes could be deleted, logs might go missing. I knew this could happen and I was paranoid it might. My police mind was absolutely certain that the quicker you got the evidence preserved, the better position you were in.

[There is no indication that evidence was concealed, deleted or lost.]

...

In August 2011 the IPCC produces a report about the sharing of information between Durham Prison and Northumbria Police [that version of the report is never released by the IPCC; it is amended in 2013 and a heavily redacted version is disclosed under the Freedom of Information Act in 2015]. The report says that on the morning you were released, one of your fellow prisoners told two prison officers that you were planning to hurt Sam. One of the officers wrote a short report saying,

MOAT was released 1/7/10 from HMP Durham. After his release I was advised by [another prisoner] that he has plans to seriously assault his partner. He also stated whatever the outcome he would not be returning to prison.

According to the coroner's conclusion at the inquest into the death of Christopher Brown, the officer handed that report to the security manager at the prison. The security manager gave it to an analyst. The analyst read the report in the afternoon, added Sam's name and address and a recommendation that it be sent to the police liaison officer, then returned it to the security manager. The security manager wrote that action was required within seventy-two hours [the other options are twenty-four hours or immediately] and sent it to the governor. The next morning the prison governor found the report, read it and decided it should be seen by the police liaison office [which was staffed by police officers] and offender management unit [which was staffed by probation officers]. The report was sent to another analyst, who finished some other work, then took it to the police liaison office at 11.30am, where it was left in a box. The police liaison officer was unaware it was urgent. The analyst returned to her desk and distributed a synopsis of reports as usual.

A probation officer received the synopsis of reports and noticed your threat so she called Gateshead's probation office. They knew nothing about you, so she phoned Gateshead's domestic-violence police unit and asked for the senior officer. She was told the senior officer was unavailable, but was put through to another officer. The probation officer explained the threat [it is disputed whether she mentioned serious assault] and the police officer, a colleague, and later their boss, tried to find more information. They found the names of several of your former partners, but no mention of violence between you and Sam. They asked the probation officer to find out more information.

The probation officer hung up and spoke to the police liaison officer at the prison. The police liaison officer found the report in the box and gave it to the probation officer, but it revealed little new information. The probation officer called the domestic-violence unit again to let them know. The officers in the domestic-violence unit discussed what they could do, but made no more calls, and finished their shifts at 4.30pm.

Meanwhile the police liaison officer at the prison emailed a report to Northumbria Police's intelligence bureau. It arrived just after 4pm. Officers monitoring the inbox left work at 4pm.

[The coroner said,

I am not satisfied that the information we have had and the information which was available, and I stress available, was used inappropriately and therefore I am not satisfied that a failure to use that information has directly caused Christopher's death or indeed contributed to it.]

...

In September 2011 the jury at your inquest is told you were hit by one taser projectile before you died. It was fired because officers thought you were about to shoot yourself. The projectile knocked you backwards. You yelped, then sat up and shot your-self. The projectile did not incapacitate you. Nor did it cause you to involuntarily shoot yourself. Another projectile was fired at you, but missed. The jury decides you killed yourself. One of the witnesses at the inquest is a man called Peter Blake. While in the witness box he loses his temper and says to the coroner,

You're not being fair.

The next day he goes to Rothbury to calm down. Peter looks like you. He's your dad. He's not a farmer. He's not French. He never lived in France. He's from Birmingham and he studied at the London School of Economics. After graduating he worked at Solihull Borough Council until he saw a job being advertised for the position of deputy town clerk in Alnwick, a small town in Northumberland. He applied because it sounded like an adventure.

In January 1972 he moved to Alnwick, and lived in a guesthouse where the owner made excellent food. He bought a Capri and started driving to Newcastle for nights out. In February 1972 he met Josephine Moat in a dancehall. Peter liked her a lot. She was pretty and had a lovely voice with a slight Geordie accent. She told Peter she already had a child and was living with her mum in Fenham. Peter visited her the next week and met her little boy, Angus. He was a happy little boy. Peter asked where his dad was and Josephine said he never visited and they'd never married.

Peter started courting Josephine. In April they moved to a cottage in a remote Northumbrian village called Longhorsely. Peter thought Josephine was perfect and she called him her Heathcliff, but Josephine quickly became unhappy. Peter offered to take her to the doctor. She said she'd already been. She said she was pregnant and didn't want to stay in Longhorsely anymore. She told Peter she thought the cottage was haunted. She wanted to go home.

Peter, Josephine and Angus moved back to Josephine's mum's house in Fenham, but Josephine's mum thought Peter and Josephine should marry. So Peter bought a ring, but Josephine didn't want to get married, and Peter couldn't live there without being married. So he left and went back to the guesthouse in Alnwick. He carried on courting Josephine, but she decided she didn't want to see him anymore. He wrote letters, but she ignored him. Then Peter found out that you'd been born. She'd called you Raoul.

Peter knocked on your gran's door, wanting to see you, but nobody answered. He knew your mum was inside. He could hear her. He lost his temper and shouted through the letterbox. A police officer came and told him to calm down and threatened to arrest him. Peter left. Then a solicitor's letter arrived asking Peter to leave your mum and you alone. Peter consulted a lawyer. He was told he had no right to see you because he wasn't on the birth certificate. He asked a vicar to intervene. It didn't work. He contacted the local benefit office in case your mum sought financial help. He got nowhere. He didn't know what to do. He told his dad he was doing badly at work and drinking heavily. His dad said to move on.

Peter hung around for another year, but then left the North East and moved to Croydon, where he moved in with a woman and became stepfather to her children. He told his new family that a red-haired man named Raoul might knock on the door one day. He told them you were his son. He used to toast you on your birthday, and sometimes he wondered whether to hire a private detective to find you, probably on your fortieth birthday, but he never tried to contact you. Instead he heard something on the radio. A man named Raoul Moat had shot some people. He knew it was his son.

...

You never met your dad.

...

In February 2012 David Rathband is found dead in his home. A coroner says he deliberately hanged himself. You did that.

...

In December 2013 a coroner holds an inquest into the death of Chris Brown. He died of shotgun wounds. You killed him.

AUTHOR'S NOTE

The main source for this book was Raoul Moat, who left behind spoken and written material including audio recordings he made on the run, a 49-page confession he wrote on the run, recordings of his 999 calls before and after shooting PC David Rathband, recordings of phone calls he made while in prison, audio recordings he made during the final years of his life, training diaries, a psychological questionnaire, his correspondence, and six suicide notes he left in his house.

Other sources included a recording made by a negotiator during the final stand-off, legal letters, business documents, medical records, psychological assessments, IPCC reports, evidence presented during the inquest into Moat's death, evidence presented during the trial of his accomplices, books, broadcast news reports, newspaper reports, and interviews.

The material was edited for legal and editorial reasons, then rearranged and reassembled for the sake of comprehension and coherence, sticking where possible to Raoul Moat's phrasing and vocabulary, and trying to emphasise the subjects that Moat emphasised. Where clarification was required it was inserted in parentheses. If an event took place that Moat did not know about, such as the arrival of Gazza during the stand-off, it did not go in the book. The aim was to stay within Raoul Moat's mind.

ACKNOWLEDGEMENTS

Many people have helped me write this book. Firstly, I would like to thank Angus Moat. When I first emailed Angus I told him I wanted to put the story in the context of the North East, but it became clear that the story was about a man rather than a region. Despite that, Angus has continued to be helpful and honest. I could not have written it without him and I am enormously thankful.

Thanks also to other interviewees: Neil Adamson, who was head of CID at Northumbria Police at the time of the shootings and who coordinated the investigation; Tony Laidler, a friend of Raoul Moat's; Peter Blake, Raoul Moat's biological dad; and Charles Alexander, Raoul Moat's uncle.

I want to acknowledge some of those who appear in the book, but understandably did not want to be interviewed. I tried to contact PC David Rathband, but was told he would not want to talk about Raoul Moat. I tried to contact Christopher Brown's mother via her solicitor, but received no reply. I tried to contact Samantha Stobbart via one of her relatives, but was told she did not want to speak to me. I spoke to someone close to Marissa, and was told she did not want to speak to me. I tried to contact Raoul Moat's mum, but received no response. On all counts, I understood why.

I have read and watched many news reports about Raoul Moat made by journalists over the years, and greatly appreciate the work they did. Credit also to three books: Vanessa Howard's *Raoul Moat: His Short Life and Bloody Death*; Ray Mears' *My Outdoor Life*; and, most importantly, PC David Rathband's *Tango 190: The Gateshead Shootings and the Hunt for Raoul Moat.*

Assistance was given by two coroners, Terence Carney and Karen Dilks. Thanks also to Martin Soames and James Theaker of Simons Muirhead & Burton Solicitors for their legal advice.

I want to thank the Society of Authors for giving me an Author's Foundation grant, which helped pay some research costs. Thanks also to the staff at the Society of Authors, particularly Bryony Hall, who took time to provide expert professional advice.

A huge thank you to New Writing North. They helped me with the book at an early stage by giving me a Northern Writers Award, supported by Arts Council England. Special mention goes to Claire Malcolm and Olivia Chapman, who have given me important help and advice ever since.

Following the research, came the writing. I have been lucky to work with very talented people over the past decade and am particularly indebted to the inspirational people at *Arena* magazine in all departments, but I would particularly like to thank Will Storr, my former features editor, who introduced me to New Journalism and cared about magazine features like I did.

Another *Arena* staffer I owe enormous thanks to is Justin Quirk, a writer who not only introduced me to the books of Gordon Burn, but also read and supported my proposal, and got it to Philip Gwyn Jones, editor-at-large at Scribe UK, who commissioned it.

Thanks to everyone at Scribe, and apologies if I miss any names. Particular thanks go to Sarah Braybrooke and Molly Slight, who worked enormously hard and with ingenuity to give the book the best chance of being read. Thanks to Jenny Grigg for designing the cover. Thanks to Amanda Tokar for guidance. Thanks to Marika Webb-Pullman for copy-editing, and being kind when I asked for parts to be unedited. Thanks to Henry Rosenbloom, founder of Scribe, for agreeing to take a punt. And thanks to Philip, a very generous editor. A couple of years ago I accepted I would never find a publisher who understood what I was trying to do. I am amazed I was wrong.

Finally, the people who have known me longest and put up with me the longest. Thanks to my friends for sticking with me. Thanks to my parents and their partners. Thanks to my brothers and sisters. Thanks to my wife's family. And most of all, thanks to my wife and children.